ABRAM TERTZ

The Trial Begins

Translated by Max Hayward

AND

On Socialist Realism

Translated by George Dennis
With an Introduction by Czeslaw Milosz

University of California Press
Berkeley and Los Angeles

University of California Press
Berkeley and Los Angeles, California

The Trial Begins
© 1960 in the English translation by
Harvill Press, London, and Pantheon Books Inc., New York

On Socialist Realism
© 1960 by Pantheon Books Inc., New York

First California paperback edition published 1982

ISBN 0-520-04677-3
Library of Congress Catalog Card Number 82-70652

Printed in the United States of America

1   2   3   4   5   6   7   8   9

CONTENTS

THE TRIAL BGINS

Translated by Max Hayward

TRANSLATOR'S NOTE

THE main action of this novel takes place in the last year of Stalin's life, a time of severe repression, overshadowed by his morbid fears of foreign and internal enemies. Berya (p. 85) was head of the Security Service, the "dread invisible army" (p. 90) then at the height of its power. A wave of anti-Semitism, disguised as a campaign against "rootless cosmopolitans" (p. 11), culminated in the arrest of a group of doctors, mainly Jewish (the "killer-doctors" in the novel), accused of plotting to assassinate members of the Administration who were their patients. This "affair" (p. 58) was expected to lead to a new series of sensational trials such as those of Radek, Kamenev, Bukharin, etc. (cf. p. 11), in the thirties. The doctors were in fact released soon after Stalin's death, though some people arrested in connection with them may have suffered the fate of "Rabinovich" (p. 112). *The Trial Begins* is a savage satire on this period in which "Abram Tertz" probably grew up to adult consciousness, a period in which it seemed that "everything in sight must be destroyed" (p. 113) in order to make sure of the destruction of the "enemy."

3

For the convenience of the reader, the following references in the text should be explained:

page 16 Yermak: explorer who established Russia's claim to Siberia in the sixteenth century. Shamyl: last leader of Caucasian resistance in the nineteenth century.

page 52 Rakhmetov: ascetic revolutionary hero of the nineteenth-century novel, *What Is to Be Done?* by Chernyshevsky.

page 62 *The Young Guard:* Soviet novel by A. Fadyeev.

page 67 Pavel Korchagin: ideal Soviet youth, hero of N. Ostrovsky's novel, *How the Steel Was Tempered.*

page 75 The verses are the first two lines of the "International" in its Russian version.

page 86 Sophia Perovskaya: a nineteenth-century populist, tried for attempted political assassination.

page 90 Victory (*Probyeda*): smallest of the three makes of car then produced in Russia.

page 96 *Dead Scowls:* the speaker means Gogol's *Dead Souls*

page 108 In traditional fortune-telling, jacks mean young men, and kings older or more important men.

page 122 The River Kolyma has given its name to the notorious concentration-camp region on its shores.

page 125 Emelyan Pugachev: peasant rebel leader during the reign of Catherine II. Suvorov: general who put down the rebellion.

4

PROLOGUE

WHENEVER I was at the end of my strength, I would climb up on the window-sill and poke my head out through the narrow window. Down below, galoshes squelched and cats cried like children. Thus, for a few moments, I hung over the city, gulping its raw, damp air; then I jumped back onto the floor and lit another cigarette. That was how I wrote this story.

I hadn't heard them knock. There were two of them in plain clothes standing in the doorway. They had modest, thoughtful faces and they looked like twins.

One of them went through my pockets. Then he made a small neat pile of the sheets of paper scattered on the table and, moistening his fingers, counted them; there were seven all together. He ran his hand over the first page and, presumably by way of censorship, scooped up all the characters and punctuation marks. One flick of the hand and there on the blank paper was a writhing heap of purple marks. The young man put them in his pocket.

One letter—I think it was an *s*—flicked its tail and tried to wriggle out, but he deftly caught it, tore off its legs, and squashed it with his fingernail. In the meantime his companion was listing in his notebook all the details of my private life. He tapped the walls, went through my linen, and even turned the socks inside out. I felt embarrassed as if I were before a medical board.

"Are you arresting me?"

The two plain-clothes men shyly hung their heads in silence. I was not aware of having done anything wrong but I realized that those above knew better and I humbly waited for my fate.

When they had finished, one of them glanced at his watch and said:

"You are being trusted."

One wall of my room thinned, grew lighter, and became transparent. Through it, as through a sheet of glass, I saw the town.

Temples and Ministries rose like coral reefs. Orders and decorations, shields and emblems, clung to spires of multistoried buildings. Ornaments of pure gold, molded, cast, or fretted, covered the façades of huge stone piles. Granite dressed in lace, reinforced concrete painted with frescoes of monograms and garlands, stainless steel coated in cream for beauty, all told of the wealth of those who lived in the Great City.

While above the roofs, amid the ragged clouds crimsoned by the rising sun, I saw a hand. Such was the invincible strength of the bloodshot fingers clenched into a fist and motionless above the earth, that I shivered with delight. Closing my eyes, I fell upon my knees and heard the Master speak. His voice came straight from heaven, at moments thundering like an artillery barrage, at others purring gently like an airplane. The two young men stood stiffly to attention.

He spoke:

"Mortal, arise. Behold the hand of God. Whereever you may steal away and hide, it will reach and find you, merciful and chastising. Behold!"

The hand in the sky cast a huge shadow. Where it fell the streets and houses opened out; the city was sliced open like a cake and you could see its stuffing: cozy apartments and people sleeping singly or in pairs. Big hairy men smacked their lips like babies and their plump wives smiled mysteriously in their sleep. Their even breathing rose toward the reddening sky.

Only one man was awake at this early hour. Standing at his window, he was looking at the town.

"Do you recognize him, writer?" the divine voice murmured in my ear. "He is the hero of your tale: Vladimir, my beloved and faithful servant. Follow him, dog his footsteps, defend him with your life. Exalt him!

"Be my prophet. Let the light prevail and may the enemy tremble at your word."

The voice ceased. But the wall remained transparent like a sheet of glass, and I could still see the clenched fist poised above me in the sky. Its violence increased and the knuckles whitened with the tension. The man still stood at his window looking at the sleeping town.

Now he buttoned up his uniform and raised his hand. It looked small and puny when compared to the right hand of the deity, but its gesture was as menacing and as magnificent.

CHAPTER I

Cɪᴛɪᴢᴇɴ S. Y. Rᴀʙɪɴᴏᴠɪᴄʜ, a gynecologist by profession, had unlawfully procured an abortion. As he leafed through the notes of the interrogation Vladimir Petrovich Globov frowned fastidiously. He had finished his night's work, the sun had risen, and now, here was this obscene character, with a name out of a funny story, crawling out of an unnumbered, battered file. Scarcely a job worthy of the City Public Prosecutor.

He had already had occasion to prosecute at least one Rabinovich, if not two or three. Indeed, there were too many of them to remember. Every schoolboy knew today that these people with their pettybourgeois instincts were born enemies of socialism. There were exceptions, of course—Ilya Ehrenburg, for example. But as against that, you had only to think of Trotsky, Radek, Zinoviev, Kamenev, the rootless cosmopolitans . . . people with an inborn love of treachery.

He felt a small pain in his heart. He unbuttoned his coat and shirt and squinted at his chest. There, under the left nipple, next to the scar left by a kulak's bullet, was a blue heart pierced by an arrow. He stroked the old tattoo marks; they went back to his youth. One heart—the one transfixed —dripped pale-blue blood; the other ached gently from fatigue and the cares of office.

Before going to bed the Public Prosecutor stood for a short while at his window and surveyed the city. The streets were still deserted. But the policeman at the crossroads was, as usual, directing the traffic. At a wave of his conductor's baton invisible crowds surged forward or stopped dead.

The Public Prosecutor did up all the buttons of his uniform and raised his hand. He felt: "God is with us"; he thought: "Victory is ours!"

The rain streamed down Karlinsky's face. His socks were sticking to his feet. "I'll give her five more minutes," he decided, "then I'll go." But it was too much for him and he started for home.

"Where are you off to, Yury?" Standing in the wet square, Marina looked improbably dry. "Chivalry is dead, I see." She smiled with an imperious gentleness and pointed to a dry spot beneath her umbrella. "Come here at once."

"Good morning, Marina. I'd given you up. The policeman was getting restless, wondering if I meant to take advantage of the cloudburst to blow up Pushkin's monument."

Marina laughed. "First I have to make a telephone call."

The rain beat down and ricocheted on the asphalt. The square was a sea of bubbles. The telephone booth was an island. They dashed toward it, braving wind and water. Yury surreptitiously dried his hands on Marina's waist. "You smell like a wet rag," she said. Before he could take offense she had dialled her number and said "Hello," with a foreign intonation. "Hello," she said again, pronouncing the melodious, exotic word with a sulky tremolo on the top note.

"Is that you, Vladimir? I can't hear you." To hear better she moved closer to Yury. He could feel the fragrant warmth of her cheek.

"Speak louder! What's that? What? Don't wait dinner for me. I'll be back late—I'm dining out."

The receiver gurgled helplessly. Her husband was protesting at the other end of the line. Yury took Marina's hand and kissed it. He forgave her everything: his waterlogged shoes and the fact that she was unapproachable. Her voice was as insinuating as a serpent.

"Do go to the concert tonight. Yes, without me. Please! I'll explain later. . . . What's that? Oh yes. . . . I too."

She was deceiving her silly, trusting husband.

11

"How did you like that, poor old Public Prosecutor!" thought Karlinsky. "She said, 'I too' to avoid saying, 'I kiss you too.' That was because I was standing beside her and touched her hand!"

"What are you so pleased about?" she asked in a surprised voice as she hung up the receiver. Karlinsky was behaving just as she had expected.

"Dear Marina, may I be indiscreet and ask you one thing that's been puzzling me for ages . . ."

"Two if you like." She was resigned and bored.

Yury had time to think: "You're a cunning devil, but I'll outsmart you yet," before speaking in an ingratiating tone: "Do you believe in Communism? And secondly, since you don't mind: do you love your husband?"

"Hell, they've cut me off"—Globov breathed into the artificial silence of the telephone, but there was nothing further from Marina. In the next room Seryozha was conjugating his German verbs.

"Seryozha! Come here a moment."

"Did you call me, Father?"

"Hard at work, are you? I've finished mine. Worked like a beaver all night long. . . . Look, will you keep me company? It's my day off after all. We'll have a gossip and then go for a drive. Then tonight we'll buzz off to the concert. What do you say to that?"

12

"What about Marina?" (Marina was Seryozha's stepmother.)

"Your mother's dining with a friend. Well? Do you agree?"

Seryozha made no objection.

"One thing I meant to ask you, Seryozha . . . I went to the parents' meeting at your school last Wednesday. There was a lot of talk about you. All to your credit, as usual. Only afterward, the history teacher—what's his name?—Valeryan . . ."

"Valeryan Valeryanovich."

"That's it. . . . Well, he took me aside and whispered something about having to be careful: 'You know,' he said, 'your son keeps asking awkward questions and, in general, he shows signs of a morbid curiosity. . . .' "

The Prosecutor paused, then, as Seryozha said nothing, asked casually:

"Is it women you are interested in, Seryozha?"

Seryozha glowed with an unbearable pink light. Just like a girl, thought his father fondly. He knew that Seryozha's sins were of a different order, but since, for educational reasons, he wished him to own up, he went on with the inquisition:

"Well, there's no harm in thinking about women now and again. I was quite a lad at your age—the brightest in the village, I might almost say . . . But why discuss it with your teachers? Couldn't you have asked me . . ."

"But it wasn't that at all," Seryozha burst out. "I asked something completely different."

"Really."

"Of course! I asked him about history . . . and philosophy; about just and unjust wars, for instance."

"Wars?" Globov looked amazed; he still pretended to understand nothing. "You're not joining the Army next year, are you? What about college?"

Seryozha rushed into explanations. No shameful thought had even crossed his mind. As for the teaching on just and unjust wars, it had originated with Marx and had later been developed by Lenin, who applied it to the new historical setting. To prove his point Seryozha ran to his own room and brought back several notebooks covered with his minute writing.

"So what I couldn't understand was Valeryan Valeryanovich's saying that Yermak's conquest of Siberia was just, and so was the crushing of Shamyl's rebellion. . . ."

"Yes," said Globov thoughtfully, "we can't do without Siberia. Nor without the Caucasus. Oil. Manganese. You know the folk-song? 'Upon the peaceful bank of the Irtysh, Yermak sat deep in thought.' Remember?"

"And when the English conquered India, they also . . ."

"You stop making such comparisons," cried

Globov in alarm. "What have the English got to do with it? Where do you think we're living? In England?"

He thought for a moment. Really England was quite irrelevant. Why England?

"But historically speaking . . ."

"Historically speaking my foot! Study your history but don't forget the present day. Think of what we're building! Think of what we have achieved already! Well, there you are— In the final reckoning, if you see what I mean—ultimately— our ancestors were right. What they did was just."

Seryozha's father was right but Seryozha felt sorry for Shamyl. After all, how could Shamyl know the Revolution would take place in Russia? All he wanted was to free his own people, it was only afterward that it turned out to be wrong, and even antisocialist as well. . . .

"Karlinsky now, he explains it differently. He says it all depends on your point of view. One man's justice is another man's injustice. But where d'you get *real* justice then?"

Karlinsky again! Globov suppressed a curse. "You leave all this hair-splitting alone, Seryozha. Karlinsky is a learned man, of course, and he's a good friend of Marina's . . . but you don't have to take everything he says. . . . Now then, let's have it all from the beginning: what other questions have you been pestering your teachers with?"

15

"It all depends on your point of view, my dear Marina. Let's examine yours."

Karlinsky puffed at a cigarette (it was his favorite brand) and watched Marina eat. A small, provocative birthmark set off the dazzling whiteness of her skin, but already her cheeks sagged a little and there was an ominous fold under her chin. She bit into a cake, baring her gums to avoid smudging her lipstick.

"Marina!"

Her face was blank; she turned it slowly, displaying it from every side.

"As we are friends—we are, aren't we?—I'll take the risk of speaking frankly. It's not for love . . ." He lowered his voice; at the next table two young men were stolidly sipping cognac. . . . "I mean: it wasn't out of love of country and of Communism that you married your husband, was it? You, who are so clever and so beautiful . . . You know that you *are* beautiful?"

"I know." She smiled faintly with amusement.

"And clever?"

"Yes, I know."

"I love talking with you. It's like eating spiced tomatoes. And the atmosphere in this café encourages frankness. It's colorful, isn't it?"

Yury pointed with his chin, inviting her to look around. One of the young men at the next table insisted stubbornly: "I adore the clink of glasses."

His friend crossed himself with the piece of ham stuck on his fork, swallowed the ham, and added: "A woman's body is an amphora filled with wine."

"Isn't it time we filled up our amphoras?" said Karlinsky. "But what shall we drink to? To the ideals you are so determined to keep dark?"

Marina shrugged her shoulders.

"I'm no good at talking about abstractions, my dear Yury."

"What about personal things, then?"

"Even less."

"I see. . . . You like riddles. It's true that every pretty woman likes to be mysterious. But it's dangerous to be too frank with you, Marina. You are a terribly good listener."

"Yes."

"You watch, and you remember everything, and later . . ."

"No, I don't always remember, but I always understand."

"I wish I did."

"What don't you understand?"

"Well, take your beauty, for example. How you can . . ."

"How can I, beautiful and clever as I am, live with my husband? Is that what you mean?"

Karlinsky froze. Soft-footed, with bared teeth, his prey advanced upon him. Fox, mink, or long-awaited silver sable?

17

The two young people at the neighboring table were now pouring out their hearts.

"Honestly, Vitya, in all my life I've never harmed a fly."

"Thank you, Tolya, thank you for your understanding."

"So you want to go in for law, Seryozha? A very sensible idea. Following in your father's footsteps? Good for you. . . . But honestly, all your doubts and questions aren't worth a kopeck. All these talks you have with your Valeryan Valeryanovich are just childish nonsense. You're not old enough to understand State affairs. Take those former prisoners of war, for instance, that you stick up for. Believe me, they're all cowards and traitors, and I know what I'm talking about. And then, what you said about wages. I suppose you'd put a Cabinet Minister on the same footing as a cleaning-woman and expect him to run the country for three hundred rubles a month? Do you imagine you and I know better than the people up above? Here you are, still conjugating German verbs and taking down philosophy notes, while they've discovered everything there is to know, they've summed it all up and worked it out to the last detail—including why you need your German verbs and your philosophy and what you'll do with them.

"Get one thing into your head. What matters is

our Glorious Aim. And it's by this you have to measure every other thing—everything, from Shamyl to Korea. The aim sanctifies the means, it justifies every sort of sacrifice. Millions of people—just think—millions have died for it. Think of the cost of the last war alone! And now you come along and quibble about details—'this is wrong and that's unfair'!

"Let me tell you a story. I'll never forget it as long as I live. There was a captain in the war who had been ordered to capture a hill. His men were tired and discipline was slack, nobody felt much like getting himself killed. Just then a man was brought in— he'd been caught as a deserter escaping from the battlefield. The captain shot him out of hand in front of everybody, sent up his report, and led his unit into the attack.

"Well, we get the report. We investigate. And what d'you think we find? The man wasn't a deserter at all. Another officer had sent him somewhere with a message, and the captain either hadn't known or he forgot in the heat of the moment.

"Naturally, we send for the captain. What does he think he's doing? Arbitrary measures! Shooting people without trial! Give him hell! Send him to a punitive battalion.

"Well, as it turned out, the captain was no longer among the living, he'd been killed in action.

"What were we to do now? Shame a fallen

officer before his men? Make them lose their confidence in their commanders? When, for all you know, it's just because he shot the fellow that he was able to control his men and carry out his orders.

"Remember, the hill was captured! The enemy was driven back. Frankly, at the time I looked at what had happened from that hilltop. And now you try and have a look at it. Well, budding Public Prosecutor, what's your verdict?"

"I don't want to be a prosecutor."

"Oh? You'll be an attorney will you, like Karlinsky? You see yourself making brilliant speeches for the defense?"

"No, I'll be a judge."

"I give in, I give in without a struggle, dear Marina. I entirely agree with you. The end justifies the means and the higher the end the more it justifies them. How strikingly you put it. 'Innate beauty is not enough, its victory must be won in battle.' So an experienced general hides behind this Renoir exterior! I'd never have known it! I'll tell you what, enroll me in your army. Beauty needs worship, the end needs means. Let me be the humble means of your all-justifying beauty. You won't regret it."

Karlinksy and Marina clinked glasses.

"Will you accept my offer?"

"I don't know. Let's talk about something else."

Marina's mind was wandering. Yury's was captured by an image from his distant childhood. The clever serpent handed a pink apple to a fair-haired Eve while Adam snoozed under a bush in paradise. To complete the picture, he pushed the bowl of fruit toward Marina. "Try a peach, Marina. One should always eat a peach after a sweet wine."

The fat cloakroom attendant bustled, skipped, and even limped out of politeness. He was much older than Seryozha's father, yet when Globov took off his hat and threw down his galoshes he fell upon them, hugged them to the gold braid on his breast, and muttered, turning like a top and adding fond diminutives to every word: "Hat . . . galoshes . . . check . . ."

Seryozha and his father went into the concert hall.

Music scores and violin bows stirred. The impresario, a failed *Wunderkind* bald from an excess of musical exertions, glided into the footlights and, almost like an incantation, carefully articulated all the honorific titles of the renowned conductor. The concert began.

Seryozha watched the orchestra as the trumpeter, who had ginger hair and looked like a boxer, blew out his cheeks and the violinists frantically waved their arms.

The music flowed. It oozed like oily, rainbow-patterned puddles. It rose. It roared and stormed off the stage into the body of the hall. Seryozha thought about the cloudburst in the streets outside and wriggled with pleasure. The music reproduced his private image of the Revolution. The flood drowned the whole of the bourgeoisie in a most convincing way.

A general's wife in evening dress floundered, tried to scramble up a pillar, and was washed away. The old general swam with a vigorous breast stroke but soon sank. Even the musicians were, by now, up to their necks in water. Eyes bulging, lips spitting foam, they fiddled frenziedly, at random, below the surface of the waves.

One more onslaught. A lone usher, riding on a chair, swept past. The waves beat against the walls and lapped the portraits of the great composers. Ladies' handbags and torn tickets floated among the jetsam. Now and then, a bald head, white like an unripe watermelon, slowly floated up out of the sonorous green depth and bobbed back out of sight.

"What music!" exclaimed Globov. "That's not Prokofiev or Khachaturian for you. That's real classical stuff."

He too was fascinated by the flood but he understood it better than Seryozha. What struck him was that the flowing music wasn't left to its own devices, it was controlled by the conductor.

The conductor built dams, ditches, aqueducts, canalizing the capricious elements in accordance with his exact blueprint. He directed the flow; at the sweep of his arm one stream froze, another surged forward in its bed and turned a turbine. Globov slipped into the front row. Never had he been so close to the conductor, never had he realized how hard was the conductor's work. No wonder! Think of having to keep an eye on all of them, from flute to drum, and force them all to play the same tune.

The conductor streamed with sweat, his jowls shook, his chest heaved hoarsely at each pause. From a distance he looked as graceful as a dancer who used arms instead of legs to dance. But here, close up, he was a butcher hacking carcasses and chopping ice, grunting out his short, thick breath at every stroke.

Louder and louder rose the music. Streams and waterfalls were no longer flowing—they had long since frozen; icebergs floated down, as if the ice age had come back, and crashed and ground against each other.

"Intermission!" announced the youthful-looking impresario in a ringing voice.

CHAPTER 2

Marina, stripped in front of a cheval glass, was going through her morning exercises. The glass mirrored the silent dance of pink, oval shapes. It amused her to watch. She moved closer to the mirror and inspected her enlarged reflection. Its general outline reminded her of a propeller: taut blades running up and down from the narrow waist. The width of shoulders balanced that of hips. In profile, the line from breast to buttock formed an *s:* the sinusoid of her torso.

She made a strict, businesslike checkup. Any sign of her buttocks sagging or of wrinkles on her neck? Unceremoniously, she rubbed her breasts, twisted her neck, and massaged her stomach. The mirror was her tool bench, drawing board, and easel, the workshop of a woman whose ambition was beauty. She neither preened herself nor indulged her vanity but briskly gave her full attention to her work.

24

It was the eighteenth of September and Marina's thirtieth birthday. Some women, at this age celebrated by Balzac, give up their careers. A woman, lovely on her wedding day and who once, by accident, made the cover of an illustrated weekly, has often spread by thirty like a melting ice. You see women walking about the streets, looking like eunuchs—waddling like pregnant dachshunds or as scrawny as ostriches, with swollen bodies, varicose veins, wadded breasts or tight stays hidden under their clothes. But Marina had no need of a disguise.

She looked elegant in any attitude—even on all fours with her tongue hanging out: just you try to keep your charm and dignity in such a posture!

She held the indecent pose before the mirror. It emphasized the graceful sinuousness of her back. It was embarrassing to crouch on all fours with her mouth open but it proved that nothing could detract from the perfection of her face or body.

Other women used their beauty merely as a means. A pretty woman found it easier to get a husband or a lover. Some wanted to breed, making their maternal feelings the excuse (how timely had been her action against so graceless an event). Others, it seemed, liked slobbering with a man in bed (poor, poor Vladimir!). But no one knew that to be beautiful was itself a worthy and sufficient end, and that all the rest—men, money, clothes, apartments, cars—were only means to serve it.

Marina stepped aside and her reflection vanished from the mirror. In it, a bunch of flowers in a vase replaced her stomach. Higher up were cardboard boxes and a plaster bust. She guessed that her husband had slipped into the bedroom while she was still asleep and piled up this edifice of birthday gifts. As usual, his shopping had been generous but haphazard—including even the plaster likeness of the Master, not to speak of sweets, or scents and other aids to beauty.

"And what are *you* doing here, old boy?" asked Marina without turning around. "Great men are not supposed to watch naked ladies."

She wished that, in defiance of the laws of physics, she could fix her image on the slippery surface of the glass forever; that even in her absence the reflection of her beauty should remain intact. But this was difficult to achieve.

Meanwhile, the floorboards in the passage had been creaking for some time. It was Vladimir, watching his wife and breathing through the keyhole like a little boy.

She stood before the mirror, naked and contemptuous. Neither ashamed nor pleased, she turned from side to side to make it easier for him to see her whole. She didn't mind. Why shouldn't he enjoy himself? It was her birthday, after all. But he had better not expect her to have a child.

Finally, she put on her dressing gown and, still without turning around, called out:

"Who is there? Come in."

"Many happy returns, Marina darling."

She kissed his cheek.

"Thank you for your presents, Vladimir. They are all very nice. Only that one over there had better go into your study. It doesn't really go with my room. It's the wrong style."

As soon as they had drunk to their hostess and wished her many happy returns, the guests fell upon their food and Karlinsky was able to devote his full attention to Marina. He sat on her right (her husband, as is customary on such occasions, was on her left) and made caustic comments on the other guests, much to the amusement of Marina and the envy of the other men.

"The political orthodoxy of our gathering is ensured." He nodded at the Interrogator Skromnykh, an old friend of the family.

Marina was in excellent form. She laughed at Karlinsky's jokes, heaped food on her neighbors' plates, helped herself to the titbits, and found time even for her husband, whose knee she brushed now and then with hers under the table. At the same time she directed the maid by a faint pointing of her lashes, keeping an eye on the conveyer belt of sauces, condiments, and wines. As a result, everyone was sharply conscious of her festive presence and ate, drank, and spoke for her sake alone. This pleased them all, including herself.

Yury bent toward her. "Do you notice how fervently the custodian of State security boosts his offspring? All jailers are fond of children, I've noticed. Thus nature keeps the balance between good and evil."

"And are Counsel for the Defense always spiteful and bad-tempered at home?"

"*Touché*. But seriously, this babbling of fond parents is enough to turn one's heart to stone. You'd think every one of them was a sadistic hangman."

The conversation was indeed concerned with children.

"Where's Seryozha?" asked the wife of the Interrogator. And before Marina could tell her that her stepson was away—his whole school was at a kolkhoz helping with the potato harvest—Skromnykh was already saying:

"My Boris, now . . ." And the cleverness of Boris, who was ten, was admired by all.

"Here's to the birth of a daughter to you, Marina." Skromnykh unexpectedly held up his glass. "We'll marry her to my Boris."

"Surely she's not pregnant?" thought Yury. One look at her impassive face reassured him. It was like the Interrogator to pair off children as yet unconceived!

Globov was surprised as well (what an eye that Skromnykh had!). Not to give away the delightful secret too soon, he tapped his spoon against his glass and spoke:

"Experienced interrogator though you are, Skromnykh, this time you have not enough to go on, so for the moment we'll adjourn the case for lack of evidence. Let's drink instead to all our children and to happy family life."

The toast was drunk.

"What is a family man? A family man is a man to be relied on by his friends, his colleagues, and the State. A man who surrounds himself with children is bound to be a good citizen. He thinks about his family, his future, his heirs; he is firmly rooted in his country's soil. He is like an open book."

Globov opened his hand, as big as a plate, and, clenching it again, went on:

"I personally am in favor of large families. I come from one myself. You can find us Globovs everywhere, like mushrooms in a field. We have been shot and slaughtered but they can't wipe us out, our breed goes on. My youngest brother is a colonel in the Far East, another runs a fishing combine on the Caspian. My sister is in Leningrad; her thesis has just been accepted . . ."

He unbent his fingers one by one, beginning with the little finger, and now came to the index finger, straight and strong, with a polished nail. This, presumably, was himself.

"And yet there are some people who preach childless marriages. You saw the paper yesterday— a whole feature article on Neo-Malthusianism. It's very widespread in the West. And even here you still occasionally come across something of the sort. One case has just come my way . . ."

Leaning across the bottles, Globov whispered to the Interrogator. The guests looked down at their food, guessing that the conversation was about abortion.

Karlinsky suddenly felt sick. To take his mind off his stomach he thought about Malthus. In every theory there was some truth: how could you let the human race increase and multiply *ad infinitum*? One day the Antarctic would be populated, so would the Sahara, but then what? Some universal remedy would have to be discovered.

Now, it was well known that the human embryo, at some early stage of its development, had much in common with the fish. Why should the country waste its potential fish reserves? In the Splendid Future, the fishlike embryo would be turned to good account. Carefully extracted from the womb, they would be conditioned to a separate existence in pools set aside specially for them. There

they would grow scales and fins under the supervision of the State, in charge of some co-worker of
Globov's. And next door to the abortarium there
would be a canning factory producing tinned fish
in vast quantities. Some embryos would be turned
into sardines, others into sprats, all according to
their national characteristics. And it would all be
strictly in keeping with Marxism. Admittedly, it
meant a return to cannibalism, but not to the con-
sumption of our fellow men as practiced by primitive tribes: cannibalism on a more refined and altogether higher level. Spiral development.

Yury had quite stopped feeling sick. Now he
was elated. Should he share his interesting discovery
with Marina? But while he hesitated (was it a
suitable subject for a lady?) Marina said:

"Vladimir, stop whispering. Eat your fish."

The needle hissed on the record. A tenor with a
cold broke into a tango tune dating from the
twenties.

"It was an autumn day, the trees shed leaves,
A weary sorrow blossomed into crystal asters."

A Russian émigré was singing of unrequited
love in a Paris brothel; and although there were no
such things as crystal asters, they all felt moved
when he exclaimed in sorrowful surprise:

"Oh, those deep dark eyes!"

31

An invisible choir caught up the refrain on a deeper note:

"Oh, those deep dark eyes."

"They held me bound," lamented the White émigré, and the chorus echoed softly: *"They held me bound."*

"Never can I forget them,
They blaze before me."

Globov carefully piloted Marina among the dancing couples. She kept time like an automaton, or as though hypnotized. She swayed, intoxicated, in surrender. Excitement bubbled in her like soda water; the bubbles rose up her spine and along her chilly neck to the roots of her electrically charged hair.

"Oh, those deep dark eyes!
Whoever loves you
Will, for all eternity,
Lose happiness and peace."

"Oh, those deep dark eyes," moaned Marina. She knew without having to look that no one in the room had eyes except for her. The dream of every man was to dance with her. And she wanted to go on and on forever, dancing to this tune of unrequited love, to dance across the world, changing countries, ages, partners, loving no one and swooning with the joy of being loved by all.

"Tonight *I* pick the tunes and the partners," she announced as she put on the record once again. As soon as the crystal asters (not to be found on earth) bloomed, she drifted off in Karlinsky's arms.

"Never can I forget them,
They blaze before me,"

hummed Yury into the warm hollow of Marina's ear.

He was himself surprised that he with his experienced heart could be so moved by a cabaret song. For all his scoffing at its bourgeois exoticism, he could not dispel its subtly vulgar charm.

Crystal asters bloomed in groves of pineapple. Well-dressed men with canes and golden dentures strolled up and down in front of smart hotels against a backdrop of romantic scenery. Kindly ladies held court in boudoirs—or was it couloirs? And all around were saxophones, and gigolos, and negligees, and gondolas. Diving into glowing crystal glasses of liqueur . . . Lou + Sue = love. Lu-es.

Marina clung to him, trusting and submissive. As though at last she had made her choice. As though she needed no one, no one in the world but Yury. As though affection—if not love— could be attained on earth.

Just then Marina changed partners. She signalled to the Interrogator Skromnykh; he darted to her side, wagging his tail in anticipation, and whirled her away.

Globov watched the lonely figure of Karlinsky with a sardonic look and turned back to the dancers, making a pretense of puffing at a cigarette. Marina danced, her face expressionless, upturned; torso, legs, arms, vibrated to the music, feet minced in step; but her gently swaying head was asleep. Moving through the room like a somnambulist, she stepped closer to her partner, stepped back, stepped forward. But her pale, set face and swaying head looked as if they had been severed from another body and took no part in all the bustle. Falling over his feet, her partner breathlessly enjoyed his moment, while all the other men impatiently awaited theirs. But Marina's face was calm, and she was absent, as if it were the same to her who had her next.

Watching Marina's dead, impassive face and the frenzied queue of men waiting their turn, Globov did not feel jealousy but horror at this public violation, before his very eyes, in his own home. To put an end to the shameless scene, he went up to the jaded phonograph, stumbled as though by accident, and knocked it over.

Yury could not sleep. It often happened to him nowadays: he remembered that he must die and he lay awake. Usually it happened when he was lying on his back.

His life was in no danger and, if he took care of himself and gave up smoking, he could hope to live another twenty, thirty, if not forty, years. But the thought of death, even though it was twenty-five or even forty years away, was quite unbearable. It was very frightening to think that he would not be there while other men lived on.

It was not the coffin or the grave that frightened him. Chiefly it was the thought that after death there would be absolutely nothing ever, ever more. He would not have minded hell as much: let them fry him in a frying pan, that at least would mean some sort of self-awareness.

As a child he had envied elephants because they lived a hundred and fifty years. (Pikes, it was said, lived two hundred.) When his father died he had had hysterics; he thought that he was sorry for Papa, but he was sorry for himself, for it was then he realized that he too would die; and for a long time afterward he questioned people about life after death, hoping that it was true.

Why had they deprived people of faith? How could you replace personal survival by Communism? How could a thinking man have any purpose other than himself?

Feeling that he was dying, that he would cease

to live that very instant, he sat up in bed and switched on the light. He coughed, and it reminded him that after *that* there would be no more coughing. His damp fingers touched the chair next to his bed; the chair would still be there (so would the chair legs) after he was gone.

There was nobody he could confide in. Everyone would laugh at him and think to himself: "I too must die." He could expect no sympathy.

Self-deception was the only way out. This was the remedy in common use: anything to take your mind off this nothingness, which could easily drive you mad. Some went in for politics, like that oaf Globov. Others, like Marina, escaped into . . . Marina! And here—here surely was his salvation! In this, the loveliest of all the women he had ever known!

Yury got up and lit a cigarette to help him get a firmer hold on his discovery before it slipped his mind. And as he blew the smoke out of his mouth, he felt alive, he knew that he was smoking, properly inhaling and blowing smoke out of his mouth, as dead men cannot do. And he rejoiced and he blew smoke out of his mouth, and he inhaled and he rejoiced again.

Marina was indeed an occupation worthy of his efforts. Long before this night he had intuitively, like a horse caught in a blizzard, found his own way out. He had offered himself to her as a means, nothing but a means to serve her beauty. He had praised and humored her, as he had lusted after her and fallen at her feet. Often she had disdained him, cast him off, as at the dance tonight. But it was only now that he could say, hand on heart, that he had made a great discovery, more significant perhaps than that of Archimedes.

Let Marina be his fulcrum. Marina, the inaccessible, who thought herself the sole end of creation, would be the means of curing his insomnia. As for the end—the end would be himself, Yury—and Yury's victory over Marina. He would turn her own weapons against her, he would use all means, fair or foul, to prove his superiority.

"Goddess, how humiliating will be your downfall! You can trust my modest experience to see to that."

Yury curled up in bed and, feeling he would now fall fast asleep, smiled contentedly to himself as he had not smiled for a long time past to anyone. He felt that he would live a long, long life, surviving everyone, perhaps even that he would never die. All the same, he did not switch off the light.

The record was in pieces and the evening ruined. Marina had been driven beyond the limits of her patience, and as soon as the last guest had said goodbye she declared war.

At first Globov parried her attacks with some

success by pointing out that a self-respecting woman, dancing with Karlinsky, would not have let him stroke her back. She then reminded him of the plaster bust, and of his vulgar speech at dinner, and of his whispered conversation with Skromnykh, which has lasted almost the whole evening; and finally, without giving him time to recover, she went over to a general offensive.

Her face glowed with fury. It was a white-hot blade ready to strike, while her whole body, streamlined like a torpedo, quivered with impatience.

She was not afraid of extreme reprisals. She realized that in war pity was as dangerous as betrayal. She thought it wrong to condemn the use of poison gas and soft-nosed bullets on the grounds of their inhumanity. She was intelligent enough to imagine how painful it must be to die of ordinary thermite.

"Indeed?" she said in answer to some stinging word of Globov's. "Well, you might as well know that there will be no child. I've had an abortion."

As after an atomic explosion, it was at first impossible to check the number of victims, or the area of destruction. Everything had been rubbed off the face of the earth and there was no one left to fight. But somewhere on the outskirts there is always at least one survivor.

The survivor got up, shook himself, and stood twisting a teaspoon in his fingers—no doubt the blast had blown it into his sleeve out of the shattered window of some silversmith's shop. He saw that apart from this one teaspoon he had nothing left—no family, no home. Gradually, as he remembered more, he realized that his long-awaited daughter had been killed in the explosion and—as he tied the teaspoon pensively into a knot—that he had been dishonored twice: once as a husband and once as a Public Prosecutor. At a loss to know what to do with the twisted spoon, or how to deal with Rabinovich, when his own wife . . . he said:

"What have you done? What have you done?" And, not to have to kill her, slapped her face.

Not to be killed, Marina ran into her room. She did not weep. Sitting before her mirror, she patted her outraged cheek with powder and stroked her lips; twisted with pain, they looked too large for her face.

CHAPTER 3

SPARTACUS was attacking. Their center-for-ward, Honored Master of Sports Skarlygin, was breaking through to the Dynamos' goal.

Thousands of onlookers, including Public Prosecutor Globov, had their eyes glued on the famous athlete and were pushing him on by their united efforts. But the will of thousands of others, who were backing Dynamo and who wished Skarlygin to stumble, fall, or even break his neck, raised countless obstacles in his path. Hence the ball kicked by his mighty foot, instead of flying straight as might have been expected, bobbed from side to side, tripping up the players and confusing them.

Globov put all his strength into assisting Spartacus. As he strained his muscles, he saw the enemy defenses weaken. He redoubled his effort and they broke. Then, carried by the headlong rush to victory, he struck, and struck, and struck again. . . .

It occurred to him that a football game at its tensest moment had much in common with the act of love. Nothing existed except the raging need to attain the goal. At any price—let it be death itself, or anything else. Only to break through, to reach. Only to score this one predestined goal. Closer, closer, quicker . . . And now it was no longer possible to wait, impossible to delay . . . "Please, Marina, please!"

Center-forward Skarlygin was close to the Dynamos' goal. Their goalkeeper, Ponomarenko, agile as a monkey, was impatiently dancing on his toes, ready to spring. The breathless Dynamo full-backs were hard on Skarlygin's heels. "Shoot, Skarlygin! Shoot!" groaned the stadium.

Ponomarenko rolled over and over, clutching the ball to his stomach. Skarlygin also fell but bounced up at once, lifted to his feet by the deafening roar. He could no longer stop, because the goal which it had cost him so much to attain was near, and thousands wanted him to win, and there was only half a minute left before the end of play. Skarlygin struck, and struck and struck again. . . .

When the referee announced a tie, Globov was upset:

"They should sack the referee. Disallowing a goal that's been scored! It's not right!"

"And your Skarlygin should be had up for gross infringement of the rules," the Interrogator Skromnykh teased him. (Skromnykh was known as a Dynamo fan.)

"But the ball went through the posts! Did it or didn't it?"

Both teams, breathless and covered with dust, were now leaving the field to the strains of the "March of the Athletes." Little Ponomarenko was bent double. The giant Skarlygin was limping. He was followed by boos and catcalls from every stand in the stadium. To give some excuse for his lost victory, he dragged his perfectly sound leg more pitifully still.

"I can understand Skarlygin," argued Globov as they stood waiting for the crowd to thin out. "You can't be too fussy in the heat of the moment. You shoot, and that's that. When the goal is in front of you, you don't use kid gloves. All means are fair. . . ."

He went on to draw various analogies between this and that, touching on politics among other things. Skromnykh listened with half an ear.

"What was that? Did you say anti-Semitism in the name of internationalism or internationalism in the name of anti-Semitism?" He had clearly missed the point.

When Globov began to explain he cut him off. Evidently, he would not at any price concede the superiority of Spartacus.

"All that's true enough. . . . But football isn't politics. And anyway, you know, I don't like getting too deep into abstract arguments. Theories are more in your line, you're the Prosecutor. I'm a practical man. Better tell me about that Rabinovich case. I'd like to understand it."

Seryozha went straight from the station to his grandmother.

"You've grown a bit, and you're sunburned."

She stretched out her hand without getting up.

"What's all this hugging about! Wait—I'll finish this page." She clattered away at her typewriter.

"How was the potato harvest? So the rain put you off, did it! I don't know what's wrong with you children nowadays. At your age we were all sitting in prisons. Hungry? There's something for you on the window-sill, go and warm it up. Well, come on, tell me all about yourself. You can eat afterward."

Granny was a wonder. With a few more like her the world would not have had to wait so long for Communism. She'd know what to do in a kolkhoz. She'd show them!

But Ekaterina Petrovna heard him out in silence and then banged her typewriter louder than before. It rattled like a machine gun. She bent over it and fired point-blank, without taking aim.

"There, I knew it—a mistake! Now I'll have to do it over again. That's you with all your talk."

Seryozha rubbed his cheek on the back of her chair, looking over his shoulder.

"Do you have to do a whole page again, just for

one mistake? Anyway, your author's no good, nobody will read him."

"What do you mean?" Ekaterina Petrovna was shocked. "You were just telling me yourself that there are still some shortcomings in certain kolkhozes. Well here," she poked the manuscript with her finger, "it tells you all about a model farm. Electric milkers, electric plows. It explains all about it so that other farms can follow the example. I'll grant you, it's badly written and there's too much about love . . ."

"I know those books, I've read them," Seryozha dismissed the book. "It's a lot of model window dressing—all lies."

"Hush! Stop it at once."

But there was no stopping Seryozha on his downhill slope. "I know . . . I've seen with my own eyes."

Then she drew herself up. Except for her wrinkles, she was like a schoolgirl, slim and upright, with her cropped hair and her white collar.

"This . . . this is . . . Have you any idea what you are saying?"

"I know . . . I've seen . . ." Seryozha persisted.

"You don't know anything. This is what the enemy is saying. Those who are against . . . How dare you? How dare you?"

Granny was choking with indignation, her wispy

hair, as dry as straw, flying in all directions. "Of course I'm not against . . . It's just life. You're like Father. It's impossible to talk to you. If Mother were still alive . . ."

He stifled a sob and became at once a very small boy. Her own, silly, motherless boy. She wished she could sit down and have a good cry with him. But she realized that she mustn't—she must stop all this terrible nonsense—she must be strict with him.

"Stop crying. You're a grown-up man. At your age we were all sitting in prisons, fighting for the Revolution."

But he was crying, his face tucked into her skirt, fair, downy hair curling down to his neck.

"You must go and have a haircut this very day. Don't worry now, nobody thinks you're an enemy of the people. But you think you know everything; you get that from your father. What have you seen of life? Stop crying."

Surprised that he could feel his shoulders heaving, Seryozha cried all the more.

"And don't tell me I'm like your father. He and I are quite different."

"And you and I?" asked Seryozha without looking up.

He knew he ought to be ashamed of asking such a thing, but since he was crying like a baby anyway, he didn't care.

"You'd better not go home for the time being. There's a row going on. You can stay with me for a while."

"But are we going to get on together, Granny? I shan't give up my principles."

"Principles indeed! You think I'm old and I haven't got eyes in my head. Well, I dare say I see more things wrong than you do. But don't you understand, Seryozha, you must have faith, you simply must believe . . . The whole of our life is devoted to this. It's—our aim. . . ."

Seryozha lay on his back and opened his eyes.

"You know, Granny," he said happily, his voice still raw with tears, "I've come to a conclusion: there's only one thing that can help us now—a world revolution. What d'you think—will there be a world revolution?"

"Well, of course there will be! How can you doubt such a thing? . . . Let me warm up something for you to eat," said Granny.

For want of something better, they went into the Planetarium. It occurred to Yury that it was, at any rate, cheaper and darker than a restaurant. Marina still refused to go home with him: apparently the moment had not yet come.

In the vaulted ceiling overhead, the starry heavens were switched on. The universe hung above them, with its billions of stars turning slowly with a slight creak of hinges, just as in a real sky. It revealed its depths, tumbled out the contents, and showed for certain that there was no God.

The universe was empty, and its emptiness was so enormous that it was unimaginable, and so purposeless in its infinity that Yury felt almost as unwell as that other time, in bed.

Fortunately, this time he had Marina sitting next to him. In the darkness, she smelled of scent more strongly than by day. Her presence assured him that he too existed. More than this, it gave some sense to the aimless glitter overhead. It reminded him of his aim and of the need for struggle; he confessed his love to Marina, as scheduled.

He spoke all the usual lovers' nonsense—he couldn't live without her, he was in torment, he couldn't sleep. Marina made no reply, but she held her breath expectantly, and he made up his mind to carry out the whole of his plan.

The main point was to pretend to be unhappy. Not that he counted on her pity—he staked his all on the effects of flattery, which he believed to be the surer means. Any woman would feel flattered at being the cause of suffering; and an honest woman must feel grateful and wish to show it. Thus Yury whispered how small and weak he was, humbling himself to feed her conceit, for she was to believe that he was insignificant only through her fault.

Meanwhile, the sky grew lighter because the sun rose. It was as large as a melon and it made the wretched planets run after it. The whole contraption was put in motion by a professor of astronomy who sat in a corner. He insisted that the earth turned around the sun and not vice versa as the superstitious and the ignorant believed.

The idea amused Yury. Presumably the earth thought that she was the sun. Let her. *He* knew which of them was the end and which the means, and who was the real sun. The sun revolved around its own unique, beloved self. The sun had no purposes other than itself.

What he said was:

"Be my sun, Marina darling. Your beauty is the center of my orbit, I revolve around it. All that is best in me is only the reflected light of your magnificence."

And so on and so forth—all about how pitiful and small he was compared with her (he—the supreme, incomparable Yury!).

"There will now be an eclipse," the professor announced in a sepulchral voice.

And what an eclipse it was! Even the professor had to admit that such an eclipse occurred, at most, once in a century. The sun vanished as if it had been swallowed.

The universe was quite dark, darker than at night because then there is a moon, but now the moon did nothing but eclipse the sun. Only the electric stars gleamed faintly. He realized that the moment had come.

Marina kissed with clenched teeth. Suddenly, her sharp tongue flickered out, stung him twice, and darted back. Again her teeth were clenched. She pushed him away. But there could be no doubt of it: here, in this celestial waste, under the extinguished sun, Marina had paid him for his flattery.

When the lights were switched on, her face was as disdainful and as calm as ever and she again refused to go to his apartment.

"Why are you in such a hurry to go home?" asked Yury. "What have you to do?"

"Never you mind." She smiled mysteriously. "You are getting above yourself. Have you forgotten that the earth turns around the sun and not the sun around the earth?"

With all the lights on, the vaulted ceiling was low and dingy. It was difficult to understand how it could have held so much sky. There was a crowd at the exit; a skeptical old man insisted amid general laughter that there was a God all the same, and a boy of six was pestering his father:

"Is the earth round, Papa?"

"Yes, it is round."

"Quite round?"

"Quite round, like a globe."

"And it turns around the sun?"

"Of course it does, Misha, they've just been showing you."

"And is the sun bigger than the earth?"

"Much bigger."

"Then it's all lies," said the little boy, bursting into bitter tears.

The scissors fluttered over Seryozha's head, twittering from ear to ear. He tried to keep quite still for the convenience of the barber.

It was embarrassing to have a grown-up man fiddling with your hair. He should be doing a useful job instead of wasting all his talents in a barbershop. And you had to sit in front of him, like a bourgeois, not daring to breathe.

Now the nickel-plated shears were snipping at his neck. It hurt. His eyes watered but he couldn't wipe them: what would the man think?

All great revolutionaries hardened themselves to pain. Rakhmetov used to sleep on a bed of nails. . . .

"Head a little lower," ordered the barber.

Seryozha bent as low as he could. He wanted to be hurt still more. Let them flay him—he would not flinch. He must train his will: suppose they tortured him one day?

A razor flashed in the barber's hand. Leaning his weight on Seryozha's shoulders, he trimmed the sideburns. Then he jerked himself up and flicked the towel off Seryozha.

"Anything on it?"

"Don't bother, thank you." Seryozha blushed.

"It's only sixty kopecks extra," his tormentor pressed him, his proud mien showing his contempt for the poor.

"It's not that. I just don't like the smell of eau de Cologne."

To buy himself off, he pushed five rubles into the barber's hand. His father always tipped porters and taxi-drivers.

Feeling the chill on his freshly shaved neck, Seryozha moved toward the door through two rows of white-coated barbers. Each craftsman held a nickel-plated instrument firmly in his hand and was dryly and methodically tormenting a client.

Click—click—click.

Click—click—click.

Mirrows reflected chins, cheeks, bald or curly heads, necks bowed, tilted, or bent back, mouths foaming with lather.

Click—click—click.

Click—click—click.

It was all very quiet and hygienic, nobody screamed or wept. But even the lamps in the chandelier were intolerably scented.

In the waiting room, nervous, unshaved men waited for their turn. Absent-mindedly, Seryozha opened the wrong door and stopped dead. He was in the women's part of the shop. Women were being curled and dyed. The reek of singed hair mixed with the lifeless smell of perfumed flesh.

Before him lay a woman's body wound up in a sheet. Her face was thickly coated with a pale-mauve paste; it ran as the cold fingers of the masseuse dug into it. Then the face stirred and the sticky eyelids lifted up.

"How did you get in here, Seryozha? Don't be frightened. Don't you know who I am? It's me, Marina."

Late at night, the Prosecutor entered the Court building. The watchman let him in at once: he was devoted to the Prosecutor and respected his whims.

"Go to bed, old man," said Globov, bestowing a cigarette. He set off down the corridor, putting on the lights as he went.

The Courtroom was empty, so was the witness box, and so was the Judge's chair embossed with the State emblem. But the room, so businesslike, so familiar to him in its smallest details, had even more solemnity than by day.

Globov liked to come after office hours and prepare his speeches on the spot. He did not think of it as a rehearsal: it was almost as if the normal procedure of the Court with its full complement of legal officers were taking place in the unbroken silence of the night.

. . . It was useless for the prisoner to deny his guilt, to try to confuse the issue and throw himself upon the mercy of the Court.

"No, Citizen Rabinovich, it is not for you to plead for mercy! Better call to mind the helpless mothers whom you have crippled. Think of the unhappy fathers who waited for their child in vain. Think of the children, *our* children, whom you have destroyed."

The prisoner was silent, so was the Judge, so was the shifty Counsel for the Defense, who looked like Karlinsky. All were silently agreeing with the Prosecutor.

While accusing Rabinovich he kept in mind all the enemies who hemmed us in on every side. That was why he hit the mark every time. It was but one step from illegal abortion to murder, and thence to still more dangerous acts of sabotage.

The enemy were uneasy. In the deep silence of the night they plotted, looking for a weakness, for a vulnerable spot. And now the lawyer for the defense, who looked like Karlinsky, stood up and publicly declared: The Prosecutor's own wife has recently had an abortion.

Marina was brought in for all to see. She was, in her disgrace, as beautiful as ever. She had a way of looking through you so that you felt like turning around—as if there were a mirror at your back and she was not talking to you but looking at herself.

Her eyes promised and drew on. But just try to come closer!—the feathery eyelashes would snap down and, always with the same passionate contempt, always with the same rehearsed grimace, the scalding lips would twist and utter: "Leave me alone."

"Well, why not, Citizen Judges, try her! Try her if you must! But don't forget the enemy who surrounds us."

The Judge, the Court, were silent; such indeed was the tomblike silence all around that it almost made you think that there was not a soul there.

Again the counsel for the enemy stood up, this time to announce: The Prosecutor's own son thinks dangerous thoughts. And now Seryozha walked into the witness box and publicly confirmed the charge: "A noble end should be served by noble means."

"Silly boy!" shouted Globov. "Didn't I tell you where your good intentions would get you? Your noble means lead only to defeat, and we must have victory, we must win at any cost!

"Try him, Citizen Judges, if you think fit. Try me as well for having been so weak. Let scores, let hundreds of innocents be condemned rather than allow one enemy to go free."

By the time Globov had imagined the scene in detail and weighed the arguments before his conscience, his speech was ready. As yet unwritten and not even rehearsed aloud, it had already in his mind the ring of judgment, of a sentence carried out and waiting only to be uttered. He stood up, straightened his shoulders, fixed his eyes on the State emblem on the back of the Judge's chair, and spoke loudly and distinctly, so that he could be heard in the farthest corner of the room:

"No Rabinoviches shall undermine the basis of our society. We shall not allow our enemies to destroy us, it is we who will destroy them."

Then he made a tour of the empty building, inspecting every passage, examining every corner to make sure no one was there; he climbed the stairs to the top floor and, like a careful householder, checked the doors and bolts. In this house he was the master because in this house the accuser was himself.

And it seemed to him that down below, in the deserted hall, the ritual he had begun continued to unroll.

"The Court is in session."

"The Court is in session."

The words echoed from end to end of the great building. On his indictment, cases were heard, sentences were passed, men were brought in and taken out.

For who was it, after all, who had uncovered Rabinovich's plot and launched this whole series of trials? He, Prosecutor Globov! Who had taken the place of judge and jury at a moment of crisis? Globov! All the others did was to laugh at Rabinovich and treat him as a joke, but he—and he alone

55

—stood up and pointed his accusing finger, ignoring witnesses and lawyers. There was nothing—absolutely nothing—until he made his accusation. This was the beginning of the whole affair.

Globov's inspection of the top floor had included the women's cloakroom. Such a room exists in every public building, including a City Court. He had not gone in out of curiosity, but to make sure that there was no one there. The room was empty and only the graffiti on the walls attracted his attention. He read them, smiled, made a mental note to tell the porter to have the walls washed down, and forgot them. But I remember them.

Behind the locked door of a small, quiet cabin in a public lavatory, you are alone, free to do what you like, unseen and undisturbed. Men usually scribble obscenities. Women are better than men: they write words of love and indignation.

"Kolya, take care of yourself. Mama."

"Peter, I hate you. I'll never be yours."

"Dear Fedya, I love you."

"Remember me wherever you are."

And scores of other sentences, all concerned with love and parting. Those to whom they are addressed will never know of them. They are not written to be read, but cast at random into space, to the four corners of the world, and only God or some chance eccentric will ever gather up these prayers and incantations.

I wish I could believe in words as do these women, and, sitting in my room no bigger than a cabin, at dead of night while everyone is asleep, write short, simple words, without ulterior motive and with no address.

In the beginning was the Word. If this is true, the first word was as beautiful as the words written by these women. When the first word was uttered the world came to life; it was like a catalogue; each thing had a label on it: "fir tree," "mountain," "infusorium." Stars and planets hatched out of the wordless chaos. And each thing was called forth by its special word, and the word was act.

"Action," the Master corrects me. "Court action. Do you hear me, writer? A word can only be an accusation. An act can only be a Court action."

I hear him.

The Court is in session, it is in session throughout the world. And not only Rabinovich, unmasked by the City Prosecutor, but all of us, however many we may be, are being daily, nightly, tried and questioned. This is called history.

The doorbell rings. Surname? Christian name? Date of birth?

This is when you begin to write.

CHAPTER 4

Only Katya turned up at the meeting near the Zoo gate.

"Where are all the others?" asked Seryozha. "They can't have got panicky? They've had long enough to think it over—we agreed on it at the kolkhoz."

"Paramonov isn't coming! He's got a seminar on Marxism at his college."

She hid her frozen fingers in her sleeves.

"I can only call it plain cowardice. *You've* come, and don't tell me there weren't classes at *your* school this morning you've had to cut. It's just that *you* had the courage."

"So did *you*, Seryozha."

She choked a little over the respectful yet warm "you." Everybody still said "thou" to her—teachers and girls at school, trolleybus and streetcar conductors. And now suddenly, here they were, saying "You, Katya," "You, Seryozha," as if they were in love. Seryozha insisted on it: the work in hand was dangerous and they must forget their childhood ways.

"Look, Katya"—he pointed toward the Zoo—"it's like the planet Mars. They say all the vegetation there is red."

It was the autumn and the leaves had turned. The gently swaying trees were a fantastic, unearthly red, and though Katya knew nothing about other planets, she nodded eagerly, her large spectacles glinting on her face.

"Yes, you're right. It's just like Mars."

They bought tickets at two rubles each, the price charged for adults, and went in.

Everyone else was rushing off to see the caged animals, and the pond near the entrance to the Martian avenue was deserted even by the pelicans who had already made off south. Only two young men in identical light overcoats and hats were in sight. One of them was poking a twig through the railings, trying to attract the attention of the wild ducks asleep on the bank. From time to time he even quacked like a duck, but his quacking was evidently unconvincing, for the wise birds did not respond.

"Sit down," said Seryozha. "It's quite safe here. I propose that we first discuss our program."

"How will the society be called?" said Katya, and immediately suggested: "Let's think of a good,

59

high-sounding name like the 'Young Guard.' What about 'Free Russia'?"

"The trouble is, Katya, we know from reliable sources that there is a spy organization abroad with a radio station, 'Free Europe.' They might think we were backing them. It's essential that we should clearly dissociate ourselves from all enemies. If not, the Imperialists will exploit the situation."

Seryozha got into his stride. He had taken off his cap, heedless of the risk of catching cold, and was waving it about as he spoke with growing eloquence. A new world, Communist and radiant, unfolded before Katya.

Top wages would be paid to cleaningwomen. Cabinet Ministers would be kept on short rations to make sure of their disinterested motives. Money, torture, and thievery would be abolished. Perfect liberty would dawn, and it would be so wonderful that no one would put anyone in jail and everybody would receive according to his needs. The slogans in the streets would be mostly by Mayakovsky; there would also be some by Seryozha, such as "Beware! You might hurt the feelings of your fellow man!" This was just as a reminder, in case people got above themselves. Those who did would be shot.

Actually, Seryozha put it very much better than this, and the only detail that remained unclear to Katya was whether the Government should be overthrown at once by force of arms, or whether it was better to wait a little, until other countries had done away with their capitalist systems. Seryozha proposed that they should wait for the world revolution, but admitted sadly that after it there would still have to be a *coup d'état.*

Katya asked for one more point to be included in the program of the movement: coeducation in the upper grades of all secondary schools. Touching Seryozha's cap, she added diffidently:

"As we're here anyway, shall we have a look at the tiger?"

Seryozha frowned.

"I mean for the good of the cause," Katya explained, "as cover."

"Very well," he agreed after a moment's thought. "So long as it's as cover."

"The Flemish masters," said Karlinsky, "painted the human body as if it were an appetizing dinner. Just look at all the cream and butter and fresh white bread that's gone into those Flemish ladies."

He watched Marina out of the corner of his eye. She was listening with an independent air as though everything he said were already perfectly well known to her. She was doing him a favor by allowing him to take her around the gallery.

The walls around them were hung with nudes and still lifes. The skin on splendid buttocks was slightly puckered, like tea poured into a saucer, when you lightly blow on it to make it cool; or a rotting apple when you touch the warm stains left on the pale yellow skin by other finger-marks.

In this riot of flesh, Marina was the least uncovered. Karlinsky began circuitously:

"Why do we speak of 'knowing a woman'? What has knowledge to do with love? Why was the first sin committed not under some gooseberry bush but beneath the Tree of Knowledge?"

Marina licked her upper lip. It was smooth and it tasted sweetish. Her foreign make-up bore out its promise of making the skin as smooth as parquet.

"The way of all knowledge, I suggest, is made up of two elements: connection and distinction. Isn't it true that whenever we get to know a thing, we first connect it with other things and then distinguish it as itself and different from all others? The sexual act, if you will forgive the crudity of the expression, eminently includes these first elements of knowledge. Adam and Eve were united in the embrace of love and at once knew the difference between them: which was man and which was woman. United, they became distinguished; distinguished, they became united. And having thus attained self-knowledge, they set out to know everything else."

Marina sat down in front of Rubens's "Bacchanalia," opened her bag, and took another look at herself to make sure. The round mirror was too small for her face and she had to twist and turn her neck to check up on all of it.

"Go on, Yury. We were talking about original . sin. What comes next?"

"Original sin was the beginning of our knowledge of the world. Man and woman, light and darkness, good and evil—until Hegel summed it all up as the union of opposites. But the basis of all human thought, its very last foundation, dear Marina, is the sexual act—the conjunction of two organs which are so unlike each other. The brain is only a cognitive adjunct of the sexual organs."

"That's clever," commented Marina without a smile. She gave Yury's ingenuity its due but was aware that a lovely woman must not seem impressed, even were Hegel to explain his theories to her in person.

"But what about the animals, Yury . . . ? They also . . . propagate, so to say . . . And yet philosophy is, for some reason, beyond them."

Karlinsky was ready for this· animals had no shame, and shame was the essence of both love and knowledge.

"Let's go and have a look at ancient Egypt: there we'll get down to the essence," he said, wiping the sweat off his forehead.

Their conversation was taking on an almost scientific character.

The animals at the Zoo were in their winter quarters where it was damp and warm as in a hothouse; heating was laid on. But only the snakes, cozily curled up under glass, felt at home. The rest behaved as at a railway station, pacing up and down, scratching themselves needlessly, waiting.

"They are waiting for freedom," Katya summed up their position. "They are longing to break out of their evil-smelling prison."

Australian kangaroos hopped on stilted legs in narrow passages sparsely strewn with straw. Monkeys hastily rehearsed the gestures of neurotic intellectuals. Crowded in their common cell, parakeets chirped away like typewriters. The elephant was confined in hopeless solitude.

Few were left out in the autumn chill—only wolves indistinguishable from dogs; lynxes like overgrown cats; and a sheep; this aroused intense curiosity. Presumably it was there for want of a wild animal to go into its cage, or else for scientific reasons, to complete the picture. Certainly, it would not be behind bars for nothing.

Katya was heartbroken for the wolves and bears. She inclined to the opinion that zoos as well as prisons would have to be abolished. But Seryozha reasoned with her: there must be victims for the sake of science, in the name of universal progress. In the future society, however, all menageries would be rebuilt, with light spacious cages in place of these wretched kennels, and the barbed wire would be camouflaged as branches of trees. The animals would feel almost free.

Katya listened and broke into sobs.

"And suppose they won't believe it's for their own good? Seryozha dear, I won't have it, I can't bear it if they arrest you. What shall I do if they arrest you?"

She took off her tear-stained glasses and became as helpless as all women. Comforting her was a nuisance—and a delight. It served him right for getting mixed up with a girl! Looking at tigers "as cover" indeed! If it were not for the struggle ahead, he would fall in love with her. But the revolutionary Rakhmetov suppressed all his personal feelings. So did Pavel Korchagin.

He felt sorry for himself—so good, so true, so ready to give up his life for the good of all.

When they went to look at the beasts of prey they came across the two light overcoats once again. One of them was talking to the leopard:

"What good do you think you are compared with a man, you zebra? Look at it, Tolya, wagging its tail and licking its chops. And it's all spotty. Nice to have it on a wall over your bed, a zebra like that."

The leopard looked at him with round eyes, childish with amazement. It was amazed to see this live meal wrapped in a coat and trousers, as neat as a food parcel. The leopard was presumably a new arrival and had yet to learn what was what.

The tiger was lying on its right side, asleep against the bars. Its back was striped all over, as if it bore the imprint of the cage it leaned on.

Every time the outside doors were opened, the big cats gazed fiercely around them and leapt up. They fidgeted like passengers at a provincial station when a train is coming in. It was close to their feeding time.

Only the tiger remained motionless, sleeping like the dead.

The Prosecutor turned over on his left side. He liked to sleep by daylight, after his night's work. When it was light, his body felt relaxed, his mind alert, and he found that he slept more peacefully.

Falling asleep was like sitting down before a television set which had not been properly tuned in. Shapes melted, backgrounds vanished, men with legs of cotton wool strode on floors of cotton wool. Friends and relatives in dreams had indistinguishable faces. Everything was out of focus. But you believed in everything like a small child. Here was Marina, and Karlinsky was saying to her:

"Neither gods nor animals feel shame. Shame is our prerogative. When Adam and Eve turned from apes into human beings they became ashamed. The

Fall meant Knowledge and Shame—you can't separate them."

The outline of Marina's face smudged and ran; Karlinsky too had a transparent look. His hands floated in the dark air, rising and falling like two jellyfish. He melted into smiles and innuendoes: "Shame is a taboo. We break it because it is shameful. What greater pleasure is there for a human being than to do what is forbidden? This is what makes us different from gods and beasts. . . ."

"You're a beast yourself," Globov wanted to shout, but he had lost the use of his tongue. The television screen became enlarged, as if a magnifying lens had been put in. In the foreground was a figure, with a cat's paws and a woman's face.

"I prefer sphinxes," announced Marina. "They are much prettier than your bashful apes."

"You are an Egyptian sphinx yourself," squealed Karlinsky, pleased and horrified. "They ought to put you here as an exhibit."

His thin figure faded into mist. Globov stood in the Egyptian hall of the Pushkin Museum. The hall was like a zoo. Ancient peoples were so downtrodden and superstitious that they worshipped lions and rams. But their drawing was no good, so they fitted human heads to beasts and vice versa.

He had no time to look at all the details. Before him, Marina, her front paws stretched out, proudly reclined on a marble pedestal.

"Puss-puss-puss," called Globov.

She crept closer. He had just time to remember, "Pity I'm asleep," and "It's a good thing Karlinsky has evaporated," when Marina miaowed and put her claws on his shoulders. Her face steamed like a cup of black coffee. He sipped the fragrant liquid and fell into a deep, deep sleep.

Karlinsky stood for a long time looking at the basalt beast. He was having difficulty with his next aphorism:

"Bestialism is punishable under the criminal code; this is meant to lessen its attraction for men."

"Whom are you talking about?" Marina came out of her trance.

Finally they went to see the French school, but Yury was silent even in front of Renoir. You might as well talk midwifery as anything else with this Isis of a woman, damn her eyes. No shame and no curiosity . . . Like an animal . . . Or was she indeed a goddess?

"I like sphinxes too, Marina. Would a man who had known your feline lady know all the secrets of the universe, would you say?"

"Perhaps," said Marina, putting on the enigmatic look proper to a sphinx.

Before Globov could open his eyes, Citizen Rabinovich popped up beside him. He was serving his sentence as a guide in the Pushkin Museum of Fine Arts. By what act of criminal negligence had he been appointed, wondered Globov. Rabinovich gave him to understand that he had orders from higher up to show the Prosecutor around (the impertinence of these Jews, all the same!). He said that after his love scene with the sphinx (so he had been watching, the swine!) the Prosecutor must, whether he wished it or not, acquaint himself with certain secret matters.

"But none of your mysticism, mind."

"Very well," Rabinovich promised.

Over the soundproof door, a quotation in luminous letters from the Master's works read:

A GREAT END GIVES RISE TO GREAT ENERGY

Beyond, was an empty space and, in the middle of it, a glass jar containing a human brain preserved in spirits. It was ridged and furrowed like the crust of the earth. Its two hemispheres throbbed slowly. Around them, a pale green solution flowed through a system of fine tubes and retorts.

Rabinovich giggled:

"It still gives me a fright every time I come in."

He poked the lump of jelly with an unsteady finger. It continued to throb as though nothing had happened.

"He doesn't feel a thing. He just thinks and thinks, inventing new ideas. Perhaps he had a girl he liked somewhere, but now he's got no legs he can't go and see her. He wouldn't get far on those ridges, would he?

"I'm very worried, Citizen Prosecutor, in case he should go mad from all this continual thinking. You know that it could mean the end of world civilization? We're worried enough about splitting some silly atom or other, but do you realize what's going on in this very jar? A cerebral chain-reaction. Explosions of ideas, hurricanes of scattered thought! One little slip-up and the hydrogen bomb would have nothing on it. It wouldn't be just our little planet—the whole galaxy would be blown to smithereens. What I'm worried about, to tell you the truth, is God."

"The galaxy won't fall to bits. We won't let it," Globov cheered him up. "And as for God, you'd better forget him, it's the idealists who invented him. But tell me truthfully now, Rabinovich, what sort of ideas does this thing produce? This brain reaction wouldn't be turning out reactionary rubbish by any chance?"

"Most certainly not, Citizen Prosecutor." Rabinovich was hurt. "Only great ideals and supreme purposes. They, of course, give rise to all the rest, according to the law of dialectics. It's perfectly aboveboard. Would you care to see for yourself?"

"All right! But make it quick—it's time I was waking up."

"I tell you honestly, I'd say the same if it were the Last Judgment. It's not for an old Jew like me to defend the work of Christ. But for the sake of objectivity it must be said that he too had a noble aim, Citizen Prosecutor."

The former obstetrician stared up at the ceiling. His withered cheeks glowed with a lilac flush.

"To put the son of man on the throne of God, to love your neighbor as yourself—that was most progressive, between you and me—for the period, I mean. But what came of it all, I ask you? What was the result? Just you listen."

A noise of hammering came from upstairs: the arms were being battered off some Venus of Milo. This was followed by a smell of singed flesh: heretics were being burned.

"Now they'll slaughter the Huguenots," said Rabinovich eagerly.

Globov frowned:

"What savagery! To kill people of your own faith! If it were Moslems now, or idol worshippers, I could understand it—there you had grave ideological differences. But in this case there were hardly any!"

"That's how it looks to you; but they, in their ignorance, thought that perhaps the Huguenots had sold out to the devil. They couldn't allow two Christianities to exist, could they now? It would make as great nonsense as two socialisms. Take our Tito for example . . ."

"Tito is a fascist, a spy, and a lackey of the Americans!"

"Well, yes, that's what I was saying: they'd sold out to the devil."

Their discussion was interrupted by a noise of revelry. An image of the Saviour nailed to a golden cross was borne aloft above a crowd raving in excitement as though possessed by devils. Thus they celebrated his triumph.

But already the medieval malcontents and panic-mongers had begun whispering: "Is this what we fought for? Treason! Degeneration! Nothing left of the great End but the means—first it justified them, and now they've compromised it."

"What was I telling you?" fidgeted Rabinovich. "Every decent End consumes itself. You kill yourself trying to reach it, and by the time you get there it's been turned inside out."

"These Jesuits of yours made a miscalculation, they slipped up."

"Nothing of the sort. They were right. Every educated person knows that the End justifies the means. You can either believe it openly or secretly but you can't get anywhere without it. If the enemy does not surrender, he must be destroyed. Isn't that so? And since all means are good, you must choose the most effective. Don't spare God himself in the name of God. . . . And as soon as one End is done with, another bobs up on the stage of history. Look,

Citizen Prosecutor! Here's another one, brand new from the shop!"

Once again the museum walls opened like a picture book. Painted angels fluttered painted wings. Globov frowned: "More clerical propaganda!"

"Not at all, Citizen Prosecutor. It's all Leonardo da Vinci. Individualism. Free thought, free personality. The very same personality that replaced Christ and was gradually to establish the bourgeois way of life. But just look at it at that early stage—isn't it an end worthy of any means you care to use? Look at the beauty! The erudition!"

"I don't want to see any more." Globov turned away, suspecting a trick.

But Rabinovich went on as if he hadn't heard:

"In the name of this freedom, one personality squeezes another personality's guts. Look at that cutthroat competition! Now it's almost time for another End. In the name of Communism . . ."

"Shut up! Stop that machine."

But it was too late.

The world of Tyranny we shall destroy
To its foundations, then . . .

Ready! Aim! Fire!

CHAPTER 5

GLOBOV had a complimentary ticket for Seryozha and they watched the military parade together.

They had a good view of the square crowded with tanks and infantry, but the main reviewing stand was a long way off and Seryozha could not see it properly.

"He's smiling," said his father, who, by some miracle, always knew. Seryozha rose on tiptoe but still could not see anything except some pale-blue patches ringed with gold. He thought his father must have made it up, but a large man behind them confirmed in a deep, fruity voice:

"Yes, he's smiling, and he just waved like this."

"Not like that, like this," corrected a bony woman with opera glasses. Suddenly her voice rose to a shriek:

"He's looking up at the sky, our bright-eyed eagle! He's looking at his fledglings!"

Bombers were flying past in close formation, and such was the grandeur of their dense, unwavering flight that you felt like rolling over on your back like a puppy to show your admiration and humility. But they were too preoccupied with their lofty, all-absorbing task to waste time on trifles and gloat over you as they pinned you down to earth. Ramming the air, they moved on to their target (Lord alone knew where it was), a target-to which Seryozha, as he realized at once, was totally irrelevant; indeed, he felt, the whole square could not be more to them than a landmark by which they took their bearings.

His father shook his shoulder.

"You're looking the wrong way. Look to your left, further to your left, look! He's waving to the crowd!"

"Our darling! Our joy!" groaned the bony woman, craning her neck to the left. She looked as if she might foam at the mouth at any moment and Seryozha felt embarrassed by his own indifference. To his shame, he still could not make out, among the blobs on the grandstand, the One whose proud name intoxicated all the rest like wine.

His name was spoken in hushed voices in the crowd, and bellowed out by the loud-speakers. His portraits, varying in size but otherwise much alike, were floating across the square like sailing ships. And as they passed before him and walked on, the

marchers, instead of looking where they were going, twisted their whole bodies around to get one
last look at him from afar.

And yet, so it seemed to Seryozha, he was himself in some strange way absent. Everything spoke
of his presence, but somehow he was just not there.

"Have you seen him yet?" insisted Globov. "Are
you blind? Are you short-sighted?"

Seryozha made a despairing effort, picked out
one blue blob a little apart from the rest, and, in
his mind, added the missing face.

"Now I see," he said, and, taking courage, asked:
"He's smiling and nodding and waving his hand, is
that right?"

"Yes, that's he. That's the Master."

Yury stayed away from the parade. He said he
was ill and spent the morning tuning in to jazz.
His radio set was German. He could even get the
B.B.C. He enjoyed hopping up and down the scale
from one end of the world to the other. Arab wail-
ing took the place of a French commercial. And
here were two programs incongruously tangled up:
a service relayed from a Scandinavian church, and
an account, in a rich Ukrainian contralto washed
with disinfectant, of the achievements of the distinguished lathe-turner Nalivayka who had fulfilled his year's plan in time for the Anniversary.

Yury's fingers throbbed. They vibrated with the

ether. Sound-waves looped and looped about his neck. And echoing in his belly and his hollow chest, the black magnetic sky hummed and shuddered, riddled now and then with Morse like tracer bullets. Yury was an aerial. But he wanted to be a transmitter sending out powerful waves of any length he chose. "Hello! Hello! Karlinsky calling! Listen to me and to me alone!"

The stations, each busy with its own affairs, were shouting one another down. They surrounded him like market women. He spun around, twiddling the knob, turning to each in turn almost without a pause.

He hummed psalms; his feet under the table tapped to a Brazilian samba. But what had *he* to offer to the world in his own name? Some potpourri of Freud and a Hawaiian guitar? Who and where was he, the one and only Yury, if the time had come for everyone to speak?

Finally he found the wave length of Radio Free Europe. Very confidentially—he must have been a little frightened himself—the announcer promised something spicy in honor of the October celebration, and passed the microphone to a former lieutenant-colonel of the air force, turned gray with bitterness and hardship in the Soviet service. But his other-worldly voice got no further than "My dear brothers and sis . . ." when it was interrupted by an angry roar. Our jammers were in action. A rattle of machine guns and artillery, loud enough to split the eardrums, swept American jazz, Paris commercials, and Radio Free Europe and wiped them out. On boundless electronic fields, the battle was engaged.

Yury skipped across no man's land and drew breath. The gunfire was dying down and giving way to parade-ground music and shouts of hurrah. The first unit of the marchers was passing the main tribune.

This was the last straw. He switched off, wrenching the knob as if he were wringing the neck of a netted bird. He even fancied he heard the crunch of bones.

The Prosecutor always called Ekaterina Petrovna "Mother." Though what sort of mother was she? She was hardly even his mother-in-law now; since his second marriage they scarcely ever met. All the same he made it a rule to call on her on each of the two holidays: November 7th and May 1st.

"Mother" laughed at him—"Well, Prosecutor, so you found nothing better to do? Had a drink to the Revolution yet?"—and gave him tea as thick as strong red wine.

A map of Korea dotted with flags hung on the wall. At the time of Seryozha's birth it had been a map of Spain. Tiny crimson rags on pins followed the line of the front. The old lady, conservative in her habits, moved them accurately every morning.

Globov yawned, expanding his resilient, be-medalled chest, and his chair creaked.

"That's really quite a paunch you've got now," said Ekaterina Petrovna. "At this rate you'll soon be made a Minister. Why doesn't your new wife do something about it? Don't get cross, I'm only joking! Well, how are things at home? Out with it. Still fighting, the two of you?"

She could not be deceived.

"It's not too good."

His peasant jowls and cheekbones, lean and angry, showed suddenly under the skin and fat.

"You know how it is, Mother, I was born and bred among people with healthy bodies and healthy minds. All this hocus-pocus, fancy intellectual stuff, it isn't my line. Sometimes we don't talk for weeks on end, we even have our meals apart. It's as if I were not her husband but some sort of adjunct to her, a means to an end. . . . I'm a plain man, I've got far, but I've come up the hard way. . . ."

"Now don't you start boasting. You've got nothing to boast about."

"With these two hands I've plowed the soil and I've sent people to their death. . . ."

He pushed his fists, like two tanks, to the middle of the table. Here they stopped, just short of the sugar bowl, turned, fell over with a scratching of cloth and ringing of crockery, and lay flat, meaty bellies up. Globov complained of heart trouble. With his blood pressure he needed perfect quiet. But how could he keep calm, with all this mess at home, and living on his nerves at the office, and the international situation not being exactly as peaceful as a health resort?

In strict confidence he told her that spy centers had been uncovered in X-garia and Y-akia. A group of criminals in the Z Regional Party Committee had been plotting to seize power. The enemy, whose insolence now went beyond all bounds, attempted to spread panic, and wild rumors were flying around the city, one more fantastic than the other—for instance, that cancer germs concealed in matches had been infiltrated into the country by a foreign power (you pick your teeth with a match and it's all over with you), or that, under the influence of cosmic rays, women were only giving birth to girls (to the detriment of our Army).

The Prosecutor's ears were flushed with blood as thick and dark as oil. His neck bulged over his collar. It was time, my goodness, it was high time for a good bloodletting, for a sensational public trial to clear the air!

The old lady wrapped herself in her moth-eaten shawl, as if she were chilly, and told a story about some people she had known in prehistoric times:

"Yes, it happens . . . Konstantin Pluzhnikov—who would ever have believed it—spying for the Japanese! But afterward it all came back to me, that same Pluzhnikov was hobnobbing with the Mensheviks as far back as Geneva. . . . Sometimes of course there are mistakes and innocent people suffer. . . ."

"Do you know what happens, Mother, when tanks go into attack?" asked Globov hoarsely and got up. "Whatever's in their way, they crush it. Sometimes even their own wounded. A tank simply cannot turn aside. If it went out of its way for every wounded man it would be shot to pieces by antitank guns blazing at it point-blank. It just has to crush and crush!"

The Prosecutor stood, his unhealthy face grave and sad. Ekaterina Petrovna got up too—she couldn't help it.

"You don't have to teach me my ABC's, Vladimir. Our aim justifies any sacrifice. But nothing else would justify it, you see that? Nothing else."

She reached up with an old woman's stiffness and kissed his purple, blown-out cheek—as if she were indeed his mother, his own illiterate, long-forgotten mother who had once made the sign of the cross over him to bless him on his way as he left the village. . . .

Already in his galoshes, on his way out, the

81

Prosecutor stopped in front of the map on the wall. The tiny red rags hung from their pins, dusty and evidently long untouched: there had been no change on the Korean front.

"But it's Trotskyism, pure Trotskyism!" Karlinsky was delighted with his discovery. It went far beyond his hopes. And these children had actually formed a group—a society of boys and girls who had taken up world revolution!

While he read the notebook she had brought him, Katya looked around the room. She felt oppressed by the amount of furniture which had been squeezed in between the walls plastered with books and pictures. There was even a real icon—not in the corner where a believer would have put it but, as befitted a cultured man, over the radio set, next to a Japanese print.

"I am glad of this chance to get to know you better, Katya. Sorry, I don't know your patronymic. . . ."

She could hardly remember it herself. So little worn, it embarrassed her like a new dress which attracts attention.

"Let us be frank, my dear. Our friend is on a slippery path. Tell him so when you hand this treatise back to him."

"You mean Seryozha . . . ?"

These girls with glasses and wrist bones too big

for them and breasts too small! And this first secret love, on an ideological basis! What more suitable material for a psychological experiment? Perhaps something on the lines of an old-fashioned play—a struggle between sentiment and duty.

He gazed fondly at a china group nestling on the whatnot: a nymph eluding the embraces of a goat-legged satyr. Her hands gave cover to her front but left her equally attractive back view unprotected. Karlinsky stroked her blue-white back with his cigarette.

"Revolution, party-maximalism, democracy in peasant shirt sleeves, vintage 1920's." He waved the notebook. "The Trotskyists argued along much the same lines. . . ."

Katya was shocked. What did enemies of the people, spies and saboteurs, have to do with it? Such men had to be destroyed, mercilessly, as was being done by Berya. But Seryozha's organization, so far nameless, existed for the struggle for freedom and for a genuinely Soviet regime. She shuddered with disgust as a newspaper cartoon came into her mind: Trotsky, or Tito, or some such mercenary killer, pictured as a long-tailed rat and surrounded by his hangers-on, sat enthroned upon a hill of human bones.

Yury did not, however, go into the details of Trotskyism. He had a more amusing task on hand. He, the lifelong counsel for the defense of thieves and speculators, would now defend the world's foremost Power.

Jerking himself up from the sofa, he adopted the melancholy pose appropriate to the defense in a difficult case. Patricides, and those who robbed the treasury, or corrupted minors, needed the benefit of pathos and rhetorical gestures. Pickpockets and drunken brawlers were a different matter. There a joke or two, a little sharpness, could do no harm. But a grave criminal had a right to sympathy. His counsel was his conscience, wounded by the process of justice.

"If I didn't know our dear . . . Seryozha, if I were not his father's friend—if I had not met you —I would . . . I would . . ."

Karlinsky's long thin shadow leapt among the Japanese prints, clasped its hands, and climbed the ceiling, arguing, refuting.

"How can you admit . . . Everybody knows . . . Either or . . . Never mind about . . . Marxism, nihilism, skepticism . . . Action, fraction . . . Left deviation, Right deviation . . . Essentially . . . Necessary sacrifices . . . Glorious aim . . . In the name of . . . Aim, aim, aim . . ."

"A noble end ought to be served by noble means," Katya protested weakly.

Karlinsky's blood was up. Trust a goody-goody who doesn't know where babies come from to fancy herself as a Sophia Perovskaya.

"Noble means indeed! Just wait and see what

will happen to you and your noble means . . .
If you were in power, you would yourself . . .
Suppose I took it into my head to become an
emperor . . . or even to blow up the Pushkin
Monument on the Tverskoy Boulevard . . . Would
you pat me on the back for that? And what difference will it make to me which lot puts me in the
clink? You reformers! I suppose you'd like to see
a kindly socialism, a free form of slavery . . . ?"
Checking himself in the nick of time, he switched
back to current forms of speech:

"Objectively speaking . . . the logic of the
struggle . . . the wheel of history . . . He who
is not with us . . . Encirclement . . . Socialism
in one country . . . In essence . . . Speaking objectively . . ."

Katya sat in dejected silence.

"Counter . . . xism . . . ism, ism, ism . . .

"Principle . . . incible . . .

"Jective . . .

"Manity . . . lution . . . *Pferd* . . ."

Katya was crushed.

Hadn't Seryozha warned her that they must be
careful not to let the Imperialists exploit them?
They always seized their chance. And now they
had. Spies and sharks, gangsters and samurai, coiled
like dragons, bloated like frogs, grinning from
posters, caricatures and evil Japanese prints—the
enemy reached out, encircled, spread his net. Who
had let him in? Was it Karlinsky, who had proved

it all as clearly as that twice two makes four, or Seryozha, who had sent her to consult this character about his petty-bourgeois program? Or was it she herself—not meaning to, of course, speaking objectively—and yet, objectively speaking, hadn't she opened the door, showed tendencies, failed to oppose . . .

"And you'd better liquidate that notebook," Karlinsky called after her. "And think it over at your leisure, which is dearer to you . . . In the name of . . . Necessary victims . . . Wait! Katya! . . ."

He came out on the landing and listened to the click of her heels echoing in the dark hall. The girl had guts. But perhaps in future the Prosecutor's son and heir would be more careful. Perhaps he would refrain from implicating the custodians of freedom in his risky games of chance; implicating people who remained free—free to think original thoughts.

He hung his head over the banisters and spat into the stair-well. For a long time there was no answering sound. The dark, stony precipice at his feet made him giddy. But so distinctly did the moist echo reach him in the end that he spat again.

Globov refused vodka: he had a bad heart. As the guest of honor, he was not obliged to drink. Sipping, out of politeness, a glass of fizzy mineral water, he alone in all that gay, exclusively male company kept a clear head.

The Interrogator Skromnykh took him aside. Covered by the clink of knives and glasses, their conversation was inaudible to curious ears (should there be any) and became intimate.

"Your Rabinovich case has come my way. He's been turned over to us. I'll say you've got a good eye, Globov. You're a real sniper! A Robin Hood! A Tyll Eulenspiegel."

Throwing a stealthy look over his shoulder, Skromnykh almost nuzzled the Prosecutor's neck.

"Remember what you hinted at . . . as far back as September? I guessed what you were getting at at once. And now we've dug a little deeper: between you and me, we've got a case to make your mouth water."

"You don't mean to say it's political?"

"You like to have your little joke, Comrade Globov. As if you didn't know . . . It was your notes that put us on the track . . . And needless to say, he's not the only one . . . It's on a country-wide scale, my dear fellow . . . Medicine! Doctors! . . . See what I mean? And all of them, you know, fellows with long noses . . . cosmopolitans! Every one . . ."

He bustled back to the dinner table, encouraging his guests like a hospitable housewife: "Eat, boys, fill your plates, don't be shy. It's a stag party, so you have to help yourselves."

Globov found he was enjoying himself and decided to stay late. He liked these people; they were Skromnykh's colleagues, everyone with a face like an open book, a past as clear as glass, and a stainless conscience. Kindly men of whom perhaps half the world was terrified.

Among them were people with special talents: a champion diver, a singer good enough for the opera, a professional whistler. Globov was the only guest in uniform, all the rest were in plain clothes; yet he knew that there were several captains in the room, a few majors, and even two lieutenant-colonels. The dread invisible army was relaxing at its festive meal.

They talked about their children, about football, and about their summer holidays. Some liked to take their leave in Kislovodsk, others definitely preferred the Crimean seaside. One of the two lieutenant-colonels (the whistling virtuoso) announced that he was buying a car, a Victory:

"I've got to pay for it in two days' time, but I still can't make up my mind about the color—beige or gray."

An argument broke out. Beige was smarter, insisted Skromnykh. Others objected that a beige Victory was common.

Globov was delighted by the absence of formality. No shop talk, no political-ideological showing off, such as was usual among colleagues in other branches. These, outwardly, were the coziest of men; their politics were all inside them, deep in their hearts, hidden in that secret place where other mortals keep their vices.

How deluded was the mercenary Western press whose scribblers portrayed these men as somber villains. In reality, they couldn't be nicer; they were witty, home-loving; according to Skromnykh, many of them liked fishing in their spare time, or cooking, or making toys for children. One senior Interrogator, employed on cases of the utmost gravity, used his leisure knitting gloves and embroidering doilies and cushion covers; he maintained that needlework was good for the nervous system. But let nobody take it into his head that if the need arose . . .

Guns fired a salute, shaking the windows; it was as if a huge bottle had blown its cork. This time Globov had to drink down his champagne, but he allowed himself only one glass.

"A toast . . . He whose inspired genius . . . Undeviating advance . . . Into battle! From victory to victory!"

The table was like a battlefield: wine dribbling like blood, pies squelchy like a military road on a wet autumn day; splintered skeletons of herrings; ash and cigarette butts; red and rusty stains.

The more they drank, the less they talked. Other people in their cups shouted and brawled, but these, with every glass and every bottle, sank deeper into immobility and silence. It actually seemed to Globov that with every gulp they took they sobered up. Fixed, owlish eyes observed, ears listened.

One young man, probably only a lieutenant, burst out:

"I went to see *The Fall of Berlin* at the Metropole last night."

Drawn as by a magnet, necks and ears stretched toward him from all sides and froze attentively.

The speaker gave a frightened squeal. "I enjoyed it very much. . . . I really do recommend it," and quickly stuffed his mouth with a sardine.

The silence was complete. They no longer even clinked glasses. Silently they drank, silently they ate. And as silently they would die, if need be.

Interrogator Skromnykh could only just sit upright in his chair.

"Who was it you asked about, Globov? What Rabinovich? Never heard of him. What's that? *I* told you? You must have been dreaming."

His eyes, crisscrossed with small red veins, were glazed in genuine astonishment.

"Good for you! That's the way to drink." Globov winked. He expected the whole unit to leap up at his words, stand at attention, and grunt: "Thank you, sir," in a hoarse whisper. But they were all drunk, and all as dumb as the fish which—among other things—they were eating.

To cover up her tracks Katya went on foot. She carried the notebook in her sleeve. Sheet by sheet, she tore it up into small scraps, rolled them in her fingers, and dropped them in the street.

She was being followed. Who it was who followed her, she could not find out, however often she looked back. There were too many people about. The road was crowded with them going for an evening stroll, or to look at the illuminations which had been put up for the holiday.

Tonight the city was like the model of the human blood system which had been explained to her at school. A human being sawn in half and picked clean, down to the last capillary vein, is seen to be made up of a great number of many-branched blood vessels varying in thickness and in color.

The city had even more such vessels and they had been dressed for the evening's entertainment. Down the glazing arteries from one end of the town to the other, chilled blood dripped in dotted lines.

Katya stopped in front of Seryozha's house and crossed the road. The two windows of his room were dark, like tombs. She crossed her fingers to ward off ill-luck.

But it was too late. The blow had already fallen.

While she was running down the stairs, Karlinsky must have picked up his receiver, made a call, and the light behind Seryozha's windows had gone out. Or perhaps Karlinsky hadn't made the call, and Seryozha had simply forgotten about poor Katya and was peacefully asleep? Or he might be out with his friends discussing Trotskyist plans. It made no difference, she could do nothing for him. And it was her own fault. She had scattered the scraps of paper and left them like a paper trail to lead others to his house.

Far behind her, the hunt was already on. They were sweeping the pavement, looking under galoshes, draining puddles, bending busily to their task.

By tomorrow, all the scraps would be collected, ironed out, fitted and pasted together. And all the twenty-four lined pages, as indestructible as a hydra whose heads grow again as fast as they are cut off, would be there in their blue binding; and there would be Seryozha's petty-bourgeois plan, scrawled all over them in his tiny writing. There to be seen. There to be judged. There before the terrible, the just tribunal.

The earth shook. Steel pipes reared into the upturned sky. This was the aorta of the city, bursting somewhere behind the Universal Stores. They should put on a tourniquet, but it was too late.

Other vessels had already burst, and fountains of multicolored blood splashed into the sky.

Katya walked home to the thunder of saluting guns. She did not look up, she did not count the volleys. Every shot seemed to her to be the last. At any moment, the veins and arteries would run dry and the huge torn heart would stop: it was having an attack. But it thumped and thumped, shaking the asphalt at her feet and lighting up the faces of the passers-by with a glow which turned from pink to green.

Katya decided that if it banged five times she would go to the principal, or to the Regional Party Committee, or still higher. She would do it the very next day. Without telling him, she would save Seryozha, she would undo the snare set by the spies, she would explain that there had been a mistake, that Karlinsky had told a lot of lies, and that all that mattered was the common good.

After the fourth bang, Katya still hoped there would be no more. But the heart stopped beating only after the fifth. And suddenly it was so still that she wished that she were in bed and crying her eyes out. After all, she had a right to cry. This was the one right nobody could take away.

Late at night, after the lights had been put out and people, tired out by the holiday, had fallen fast asleep, two plain-clothes men came out into the empty streets. Strolling about the district allotted to them from above, they dreamed dreams and conversed in a low voice, heart to heart. One was called Vitya, the other Tolya. It is not given to us to know more than this.

"Look, Vitya," said Tolya, "isn't it time the sewage system was made to do some real work? Think of all the secret material that gets flushed away without the least control! Plans, surveys, love letters, drafts of literary works, and sometimes even finished copies!

"They say the writer Gogol, who lived in the nineteenth century, burned one of his poems in his stove; it was called *Dead Scowls*. And to this very day, nobody knows what was in it.

"Well, nowadays there's central heating so nobody can burn anything. Nowadays they all try to tear their secrets up into little bits and flush them down the drain, so as to remain incognito. That's what we must attend to.

"Couldn't we, for instance, put a special dragnet, or a sieve, underneath each house and give the porter strict instructions to extract all papers that have writing on them? Genuine impurities—toilet paper, newspapers—those could be left alone. Leave them free to go anywhere they like. What d'you think of that, Vitya? Is it an idea?"

Vitya remained silent, looking around him

94

thoughtfully at the deserted neighborhood. Finally he said gently:

"It isn't scientific to dig up every bit of dirt. Frankly speaking, I'm not interested in Gogol. I'm interested in another writer, he's called H. G. Wells. Have you read *The War of the Worlds* or *The Invisible Man?*"

"No, I haven't," Tolya owned up sadly.

"Well, I know his *Time Machine* almost by heart. But what I'm interested in is another discovery. Also out of science fiction. It's an apparatus called a psychoscope. Rather like your dragnet, only more thorough. It's so that you can tell what people think about and feel. So that even those who don't say anything and who don't put down their thoughts in writing should be automatically subject to control. At any hour and at any distance. What d'you think of that?"

"What did you say it was called, Vitya?"

"A psychoscope."

"Yes. It makes you think."

Both fell silent and dreamed their dreams. But they dreamed in concord. They dreamed about the same thing. It was this:

In our age, the age of television and of radar, the epoch of atomic energy applied to peaceful ends, it would be excellent to have a psychoscope in every district. Say, for instance, that I'm a harmful element and I'm sitting in my under-populated apartment, knowing in advance that every one of my ideologically negative thoughts, each and every criminal plan I make, is projected on a screen at the District Psychoscopic Point, just as at the movies! I try, of course, to think of nothing. I see to it that all my thoughts are innocent—about drink, or women, or even about how to work for the good of the people. But all the time I'm simply itching with criminal thoughts. I turn and twist in my chair, I do problems in arithmetic to keep my mind busy.

Nothing doing! Before I know where I am, an evil thought has popped into my head. For instance, how might I learn to think invisibly? I fight it off with everything I have—geometry, differential calculus, Old-Slavonic verbs; I recite Lermontov's poem, "I Walk out on the Road," four times running. But that filthy thought creeps back and now there's another with it: how can I start a new revolution? And at that point they pounce.

"Good morning, citizen. What was that you were mulling over four minutes and seventeen seconds back? All is known to us. If you don't believe it, we'll show you the film."

"I can't deny it," I say, "I'm guilty. I am the contemptible hireling of a certain foreign Power. Ever since my childhood I've been thinking of restoring capitalism and blowing up railway bridges."

Silence. Two men in plain clothes stroll through

the city streets. Two men in plain clothes. Slowly, decorously, they advance along the sleeping streets, peering into lifeless windows, gateways, doors. There's nobody. One is named Vitya, the other Tolya. And I am frightened.

CHAPTER 6

Eᴠᴇʀʏ day, in spite of the winter frost,
Ekaterina Petrovna, wearing felt boots and a cap
with ear flaps, called at the Prosecutor's office for
news. Her frequent visits were tactless, but Globov
could not make up his mind to tell her so straight
out. Since Seryozha's arrest the old woman had become quite impossible. She found fault and nagged
more than ever before. And each time she came,
Globov's secretary announced with a respectful
smirk on his face:

"That elderly person is here again. The one in
felt boots. Shall I show her in?"

Now, as usual, Globov's former mother-in-law
was pacing up and down his room and grumbling:

"It's not possible. I don't believe it. He's neither
a spy nor a saboteur."

And Globov tried again (as so many times before):

"Did they find any criminal evidence when they searched his things?"

"Nothing, nothing at all."

Ekaterina Petrovna's boots left dirty puddles spreading on the parquet. After she had gone, Globov locked his door and wiped the floor with his own hands, using a rag which he had brought from home and kept under the cupboard.

Then he dialled Skromnykh's number and said: "Globov here. Any news?"

Skromnykh said dryly: "Nothing so far," and hung up. This happened every day.

Every day when he came home from the office, Yury washed his hands and this gave him pleasure. It always pleased him to see dirty, soapy water: the dirtier it was as it ran into the plug-hole the more pleasure it gave him. He thought that something similar must be experienced in confession.

If Marina came he would touch her face with clean fingers. He would touch her lips. He soaped his hands again on the chance that she might come today.

In the past few months his every gesture had been calculated. The distant goal, as he approached it, absorbed him utterly. He lived only to possess Marina. He even ate and slept with an ulterior motive: to keep up his strength for his meeting with her. He brushed his teeth as if in preparation for a kiss. And now day followed day only to give her time to miss him and, after a decent interval, to give in.

Someone knocked. He waited for his knees to stop shaking and flung the door open.

It was not Marina. The woman from next door tried to push her way in as she handed him a letter and said in a voluptuous whisper:

"A girl left this for you. A very young girl like a budding rose."

Marina would be flattered, he must tell her. He slit the envelope.

"Comrade Karlinsky.

"You have treacherously denounced Seryozha Globov. He is not a Trotskyist, he's an honest revolutionary, unlike you who are a coward and a stinker."

Yury turned the note this way and that, looked again inside the envelope, and, finding nothing else, put it aside for his collection. At a suitable moment he would tell Marina, it would make her laugh.

Then he washed his hands, like Pontius Pilate. He did not wish to be reminded of Katya and Seryozha. Probably Pontius Pilate did not give much thought to Jesus Christ when he went to have his wash. He too may have had a purpose, unknown to the Evangelists.

After he had dried his hands, finger by finger, he turned to face the door and stamped his foot.

"Well, Marina, what are you waiting for? I'm expecting you. I'm ready."

The Interrogator was doing embroidery on canvas. The design for the tea-cloth had been chosen carefully and was elaborate: ingeniously twisting tulips on a black ground. . . . Every time Seryozha was brought in he gathered up the silk skeins scattered on the desk, rolled up his needlework, locked it in his safe, and opened a friendly conversation. So far all had been going well.

"Yes, that's a most intelligent observation. It can't be denied. The people at the top take a lively interest in such opinions. . . . And how about collective farms, what should be done about them? That's another of those things . . . As you know . . ."

Listening to Seryozha's views on collective farms, he sighed dejectedly. Sometimes he argued, sometimes he agreed; and so they made progress.

"And then, frankly, you know, the press . . ."

Seryozha was quite ready to contribute his ideas on the press as well, and was only puzzled why he had not yet been released.

"Well, young man," the Interrogator said at last, "now we have been into your views in detail. One thing I'd like to get straight—how did you manage to get in touch with foreign agents?"

His expression was altogether kindly and encouraging, as much as to say: "Don't be shy. Come on, out with it. We all understand. As if it mattered!"

"What kind of idiotic joke is that?" Seryozha paled. "Please remember, I have not so far been condemned, I am only on trial."

The Interrogator looked amused and drew the curtain back. The daylight was so clean and so transparent that you felt like taking a deep breath of it.

"Come here. D'you hear me? It's you I'm talking to."

"Now he's going to strike me," thought Seryozha, his face stiffening.

"Look through the window."

Seryozha saw the square which he had often crossed in the old days, tiny people diving through the entrance to the subway, others travelling in toy cars and trolleybuses, all free to go where they pleased. Snow, real snow, was coming down on them out of the sky.

"That's where they are, the people who are on trial. See how many of them?"

The Interrogator pointed at the crowds milling below. Then he stroked Seryozha's shorn head and explained gently:

"You're different now, my boy. You're not on trial, you're condemned."

It was useless to make a fuss. Globov had already had a hint from high up:

"Better keep right out of it. You needn't worry, nobody distrusts you. But we don't advise you to intervene on his behalf. You can't touch pitch without getting tarred. Better forget him and get your wife to have another while you can. As for this one—he's no son of yours any more."

But Granny would not keep quiet:

"You must insist! You must go on trying! Is he your son or isn't he?"

His son! Other people's children were . . . just children. They graduated. They went in for law. It was true that Skromnykh's boy had been in trouble, but that was only for theft. His father gave him a hiding to teach him a lesson, and that was that. But this! Straight from school to prison! Dishonoring his father's name! And at such a time!

"No, Mother," said Globov, his eyes on her wet felt boots. "There's a big roundup going on. . . . I can't . . .

"What did you say? Afraid? Have I ever been afraid of anyone? They were all afraid of me. . . . No, but I am a prosecutor and my conscience won't let me. Think of all the people I see every day, people who are still less guilty and whom I have to . . .

"What future? Whose heirs? Mine? I'll manage without. No traitor can be a son of mine.

"What nonsense! Really, what has the word of honor of a revolutionary woman to do with it? It sounds a bit old-fashioned, Ekaterina Petrovna. And we have certain information.

"Oh, no! You're wrong there. It's no joke to lose a son. . . .

"That's enough! What about yourself . . . What about your brother, your own brother, do you happen to remember? He skipped abroad and I suppose you . . .

"It didn't surprise me. I had an idea . . . But if I'd known to what length . . .

"Have you gone clean out of your mind, you crazy old woman? I did *not* denounce him. Do you hear? I did *not*.

"Leave me alone. Stop clutching at me. Will you keep your hands to yourself . . .

"I told you who gave him away. A girl who belonged to his own group. One of the teachers told me. The fellow who teaches history. She went to the principal . . . as if to ask his advice . . . He wanted to hush it up, but . . .

"But it was a girl, I tell you. Don't you understand plain Russian? A schoolgirl.

"Well, you know, that's going a bit too far. I've never yet strangled any little girls or boys. But when it comes to enemies, of course, that's another matter. . . .

"Shut up, you old witch, before you are put

away yourself! After this I never want to . . .

"Very good, and what then? So you did look after me for twenty-five years? I've had quite enough of your bullying.

"You needn't. I'll be very glad if you never come again."

After the old woman had gone, he waited a few moments to get his breath, then he called for his secretary and said in the offhand tone used of outsiders:

"Send the cleaner in, tell her to wipe the floor. That citizeness made such a mess with her felt boots, the place is like a pigsty."

The telephone bell rang. Marina put down her cards (she had been getting out a complicated patience) but did not lift the receiver. Bending over the telephone, she listened curiously to its long-drawn-out peals.

Suddenly it seemed to her that the receiver quivered: at any moment now it would jump off its horned stand and Karlinsky's angry voice would twang at her from the tabletop.

"So you're hiding, are you? You don't care to come? Well, it's all off as far as I'm concerned!"

The possibility seemed so real that she left the room and went on listening next door, invisible and safe.

"How he's suffering, poor man, how much he

needs me!" she thought, starting pleasantly at each new peal.

For three months Yury had been threatening to leave her. Either she must give in or they must part. When she protested that she wished neither, he gave her a fortnight "to get over her whims" and kept away, pestering her over the telephone and terrifying her with the thought of loneliness. The fortnight was nearly over.

The telephone, after giving her a headache, had stopped in dudgeon, and Marina went back to her sofa, to her hesitations and her cards. The two were connected. The cards predicted tears, letters, long journeys, and government apartments; two unidentified jacks promised an agreeably busy time, but the kings evaded her, one after the other.

Marina did not believe in cards, but it was true that recently her husband had seemed absent. He had stopped boring her with talks on family life and on the mutual understanding essential between wives and husbands. He vanished for whole evenings on end and seemed to have forgotten that, although they had quarrelled, they were still sharing the same apartment.

To make things worse, Seryozha had been picked up, and from that day on, not a man of her acquaintance had been near her. Even Skromnykh kept away.

The king of spades was the only one left. She

couldn't simply let him go. Who else showed such royal generosity in his understanding of her beauty? And what was beauty without scenes and declarations of love?

"You are my goal, my god," Yury often said, arguing with characteristic erudition that a lofty end had need of means, however humble and unworthy, and that God, who unfortunately did not exist, would be very lonely if he hadn't thought of creating man to worship him and serve him in other ways.

Yes, it was true. Wasn't a woman the loneliest being in the world? Was there any loneliness more bitter?

The front door banged and Globov's noisy footsteps sounded in the hall.

"You're in!" he said in a surprised voice when Marina called out to him. "I wanted some money, I was going to send a messenger across, but my secretary tried to ring you up—he rang and rang for about ten minutes but there was no reply."

"I was asleep," she lied automatically and without sufficient thought, for her husband knew how lightly she slept. It would have been more convincing to say that she had been out for a walk or shopping. But Globov said nothing and, instead of stopping at her door as had been his habit, marched straight past it. The key clicked in the door of his study: he had locked himself in.

It was then that she realized that Karlinsky would not ring her up either today or tomorrow. Perhaps he no longer expected her to come. Perhaps he no longer even wished her to make the disgusting surrender on which he had insisted.

She went up to her mirror and, seeing her injured face, which looked older day by day, she almost burst into tears, but she remembered in the nick of time that she must not: crying gives you wrinkles.

That night Globov got drunk. It is true that neither the cognac nor the vodka went to his head, but he felt such tenderness in his heart that he began to walk up and down his room softly singing a lullaby.

> *"Hush-a-bye, baby,*
> *I'll sing you a song."*

These were the only words.

There was no harm in it. No one heard him, no one saw him. He was alone.

His arms, folded on his breast, hugged and carried him. Globov loved his large, awkward trunk and he was rocking it to sleep. He felt cozy with it, familiar as it was and long unwashed. Snug in his shirt, it gurgled gratefully, swaying to the tune.

> *"Hush-a-bye, baby,*
> *I'll sing you a song,*

I'll sing you a song,
I'll sing you a song."

It could go on and on, perhaps even forever.

And now there seemed to be a little girl in his arms—it was his small, unborn daughter.

Sleep, my darling, sleep, my baby, he urged her, patting the small warm back. There's nobody for you to play with, that's the trouble. Seryozha isn't at home. He's let us down, he's left us. He's a stranger to us, our Seryozha. He is a bad boy.

To get her off to sleep more quickly, Globov began to sing all the songs he knew to the same lullaby tune. For some reason, they were all war songs, and he frequently got out of tune and gave his rocking too soldierly a swing.

He was interrupted. Marina's voice rose shrilly in the corridor. He put the baby down on the sofa, tucked it up in his tunic, hid the bottles under the table, and unlocked the door.

Marina understood at a glance. But to stay in the bedroom by herself was still more frightening.

"Let me in, Vladimir. I can't sleep. I'm frightened by myself without you." Her teeth chattered with cold and humiliation. But he stood before her, dishevelled, dressed in nothing but his shirt and pants, his huge, spreading body barring her way.

Marina called him pussycat and popsy (how could he be a popsy or a pussycat? He was a prosecutor). She begged him to let her sleep on the

109

sofa (so she was already on to it!) and promised not to scold him for making such a row—he could be heard from one end of the apartment to the other. She took his hands, as heavy as oars, and, opening her dressing gown, pressed them to her breasts and sides. Overcoming her revulsion, she stroked her body with his hands, but they fell back indifferently as soon as she let them go. Then she tried to push him out of her way and enter the room by force, but Globov pushed her back, stepped forward, and locked his door.

The bottles were safe, but there was no baby inside his tunic. He must have hugged her too tight when he was rocking her and accidentally squashed her. Or, more probably, she had been kidnapped while Marina was there.

Of course! How could he be so slow? It was all Marina's doing! She had already killed his daughter once and now she was trying again, the slut. That's why she had made up to him and wanted to lie on the sofa—naturally, the sofa!

But he had seen through her, and so she had brought in the killer-doctors led by Rabinovich himself. While she used her charm on him they, the white-coated killers, trampling underfoot the sacred name of science, had done their dirty work behind his back.

Someone was sitting motionless inside the cupboard. Globov took his short sword down from the wall—a real Caucasian sword, engraved with the owner's name and presented to the Fourth Cavalry Guards as a token of esteem.

The cupboard split at a second blow. Glass tinkled, splinters flew, and plaster fell down from the walls. The enemy, escaping by means of a trick, hid in the cracks and dug himself in in corners.

It was useless for Marina to scream at the door, telling him to stop his disgraceful performance, threatening to leave the house, to take a lover, to commit suicide, to report him to the Party Organization as an alcoholic. Nothing doing, he wasn't such a fool as that! The whole world knew about her tricks now! Filled with fury and elation, he went on chopping, tearing, slashing at whatever came to hand. He spared neither Karelian pine, nor crystal, nor down cushions. Of what use was all this junk? When the enemy is within your doors, everything in sight must be destroyed, and the house itself, with the enemy inside it, must be rubbed off the face of the earth.

Glancing off the wall, the sword struck his head and smashed the chandelier. But even in the darkness, and streaming with blood, he went on beating the air, beating the empty space, hitting at whatever gave *them* cover.

His work done, the Prosecutor went up to his desk, scored and slashed all over. There by the window loomed the plaster bust which, by a miracle, had remained intact. The Prosecutor sheathed his sword and made his report:

"Master, the enemies are in flight. They have killed my daughter and seized my son. My wife has betrayed me and my mother has cast me off. But I stand before you, wounded and forsaken as I am, and say:

"Our goal is reached. We have conquered. Master, hear me! We have conquered! Do you hear me?"

CHAPTER 7

THE Master was dead.

The town seemed empty as a desert. You felt like sitting on your haunches, lifting up your head, and howling like a homeless dog.

Dogs who have lost their masters stray about the earth and sniff the air in anguish. They never bark, they only growl. They keep their tails between their legs, or if they do wag them they look as if they were crying.

When they see a human being coming, they run aside and gaze at him longingly—is it *he* at last?— but they don't come near.

They wait, they are forever waiting, gazing, longing: "Come! Come and feed me! Come and kick me! Beat me as much as you like (but not too hard, if you please). Only come!"

And I believe that he will come, just and chastising. He will make you squeal with pain, and leap, tugging at your chain. And you will crawl to him

113

on your belly, and gaze into his eyes, and lay your tousled head on his knees. And he will pat it and laugh, and growl reassuringly in his cryptic master's dialect. And when he falls asleep, you'll guard his house and bark at the passers-by.

Already, you can hear a whine here and there: "Let's live in freedom and enjoy ourselves, like wolves."

But I know, I know only too well, how they guzzled in the past, these mercenary creatures— poodles, spaniels, pugs. And I don't want freedom. I want a Master.

Oh, the misery of a dog's life! How shall I ever satisfy my sharp hunger, for years denied?

How many lost, homeless dogs wandering about the world?

Oh, bitches with almond eyes and thin sharp muzzles. Oh, angry, lonely dogs who have seen so much.

He was washed, embalmed, and placed upon a pedestal.

Countless thousands came to gaze at him and take their leave. The crowds poured out of every street into the narrow passage between the houses; there they stuck.

The passage was the way out to where the dead body rested, watched by guards and surrounded with flowers.

But the way was barred. Orders were awaited. They had not come because the one who always gave the orders now lay dead.

The huge square, trodden by countless feet, became too small. There was no room for all who wished to take their leave and gaze. Yet more and more arrived with every passing minute. And when at last the narrow passage was thrown open, it was too late. Someone, delighted at the chance to stretch his lungs, yelled in a ringing voice:

"We've been had, lads! It's all up with us."

And the stampede began.

The window was curtained and the lamp extinguished, as Marina had insisted. As his sense of sight shifted to his fingertips, Yury felt as if they blinked.

Undressing her, he could contemplate the immense complexity of her architecture: arches, apses, cupolas. Onion domes like breasts, a reversed ogive like a belly sharpening downward to the groin.

But the guitar predominated: shoulders, waist, pelvis. No wonder Picasso had such a liking for guitars and violins: their shape was that of the cross section of a woman's body.

But desire he had none.

Yury reminded himself of his impatience in the pursuance of his aim, of the means he had used to reach it. . . . But he had no desire.

Suppose it really came to nothing? He became alarmed, knowing that he must not be nervous, that a man in such a case must be as confident as a conjurer of whom wonders are expected. More and more alarmed at his own nervousness, he clutched at the apses, domes, and arches set out before him, imploring his weak flesh, which had so stupidly, so shamefully, betrayed him at the very last moment, to grant him, if not passion, then at least a little lust.

The bed springs thrummed like a guitar.

Finally, calling to mind the pornographic postcards he had long kept in a hidden place, and listing their obscenities in his mind, he clenched his teeth and made a despairing effort as if to lift a ton weight.

The ideally constructed woman lay beside him motionless, leaving him to sweat to his heart's content. With all his wasted soul, with all his flesh worn out by fruitless labors, he detested her—the unattainable attained—and dreamed only of the moment when he could throw her out (how gladly) as soon as this was possible.

"Well, have you reached your goal?" Marina asked, amused. "Why so slow?"

Yury closed his eyes in silence, though closing them was quite useless in the pitch-black room.

The Prosecutor never clearly understood how it could have happened. He had been standing decorously with the others, waiting to go through, when all at once he realized that he was being swept on by the crowd gyrating in a spiral across the square into the passage narrow as a trench.

The passage led straight through to the center of the town, where the dead Master's body rested on a pedestal surrounded by flowers. So the Prosecutor did not resist the pull but helped all he could; though to move your feet in this crush was as difficult as talking with your mouth full.

But the quicker and the closer he approached the goal, the more he was carried to one side; the spiral, winding itself up, swept him off his feet.

People were scrambling over one another, stumbling, falling. Where one had been knocked down six others took his place and the struggle continued. Everybody strove eagerly to get inside the narrow, trenchlike passage.

The Prosecutor was too stout to take part in the scuffle. He neither scrambled, nor pushed, nor swore. But a mighty hand as big as the square snatched his body, squeezed him so that he almost choked, and, slightly lifting him above the ground, cudgelled to right and left.

"Let me go! You're hurting!" sobbed the Prosecutor. "These are our own people, they've done no harm. There are many women among them, and children, and even crippled servicemen who brought you glory."

But the prehensile fingers had him in a death

grip. Using him as a bludgeon, grieving and embittered, the hand struck and struck at the mob howling with pain.

There was no hurry to go anywhere. Marina stood by the newspaper kiosk; the papers were in mourning and looked like women with heavily made-up eyes. She turned her back on the monotonously busy street and peered into the unlit window of a beauty shop. There she saw herself as in a distorting mirror. People walked across her, trolley-buses drove past, and flasks of scent and pyramids of colored soap drove through them.

"All these beauty preparations only spoil your skin," she thought as she looked sulkily at her image. But her face, smudged with shame and temper, trodden by the shadows of the passers-by, remained beautiful enough.

"Tomorrow I'll try that Argentinian lipstick," she decided.

By crawling underneath a truck and climbing over the railing which fenced off the boulevard, Globov managed to escape, though he grazed his shins and lost his hat. The boulevard was spacious and deserted.

Shouts came from behind him:

"A little girl! A little girl has been crushed!"

In the darkish passage were others who had

slipped away. Happy to have got off cheap, they kept worrying about some girl:

"Crushed! Trodden down!"

"That wasn't mine. Mine fell down on her own. Nobody trod her down. And her glasses had been broken before I got there, and she wasn't a little girl, she was of age."

"A little girl, a little girl," voices in the crowd insisted stubbornly. "Stop the man who did it. . . . She fell under the truck. . . . What are you gaping at? Get the man, get the man!"

"If it's mine, it was her own fault. People shouldn't get under one's feet. I fell down myself. Nobody has done anything. Victims are unavoidable. But then—it's for the Aim."

He was at the end of his tether. He lay down to rest on the snow as white as milk fresh from the cow. Just behind the snowdrift at his back they were still looking for the guilty man and discussing the unknown girl:

"Who knows, perhaps it was a spy or a saboteur who did it, an enemy of the people. Who arranged this crush, anyhow? Why aren't the police here? Where's the Interrogator? Where's the Public Prosecutor? They ought to be tried, people like that."

EPILOGUE

At the bottom of a small hill near the bank of the River Kolyma, we were digging a ditch, Seryozha, Rabinovich, and I.

I had come to the camp later than the others, in the summer of '56. The contents of my story, finished except for the Epilogue, had become known to some highly placed officials. As could be expected, the cause of my downfall was the dragnet mentioned earlier, which had been fixed inside the big sewage pipe underneath our house.

The rough drafts I had conscientiously flushed down the drain every morning went straight to the Interrogator Skromnykh's desk. The important personage whose instructions I had carried out, though perhaps not altogether faithfully, was by this time dead and his personality was, indeed, undergoing a wide-scale public re-evaluation. Nevertheless I was accused of slander, pornography, and giving away State secrets.

I had no defense: the evidence was to hand. Besides, Globov, who was called as a witness, produced documents which proved my guilt conclusively and in full. In the course of the interrogation it was established that everything I had written was pure invention, the product of a morbid and ill-intentioned mind.

Another failing, gravely criticized, was that my positive heroes (Counsel for the Defense Karlinsky, Prosecutor Globov, the housewife Marina, the two plain-clothes men, etc.) were not portrayed in all the fullness of their many-sided working lives, but maliciously presented to the reader in their least typical aspects. As for the negative characters—the child-murderer Rabinovich, the saboteur Seryozha and his accomplice Katya, who had become aware of her mistakes too late and was therefore trampled underfoot by an indignant public—it is true that in my slanderous story they were punished as they deserved, but the reactionary basis of their motivation was not fully revealed.

Not venturing to hope for clemency, I begged only to make some corrections, at least in an Epilogue, where, taking the above criticisms into account, I would show my characters in a more fitting light. I was allowed to do so, but not to take time off from my general re-education, nor from the trench-digging which formed a part of it at Kolyma.

Soon after I arrived I teamed up with Seryozha and Rabinovich. We succeeded without much difficulty in being put into the same hut and under common supervision. The amnesty had virtually emptied the camp of its inmates. Only some ten thousand of us, dangerous criminals, were left. The authorities, now more lenient, allowed us to form a shock unit of three, under a special guard with a machine gun in good working order.

It must be said, however, that the only shock worker in our team was Seryozha, who thought it an essential duty to co-operate in the effort to bring the Glorious Future nearer. Owing to our age, Rabinovich and I lagged behind him.

Seryozha did his fervent best to instill into us the basic principles of the new ethic. Our daily bread ration of four hundred grams each was pooled and entrusted to Rabinovich until dinnertime, when it was again divided into three equal parts.

What was the point of this, I asked. We still got our four hundred grams each or, rather, a little less, because Rabinovich secretly nibbled a small piece off each of our portions.

"That's all right," Seryozha reassured me. "What matters is not the ration itself but the principle of equal distribution of all material goods."

One day, as I was scratching the frozen earth

with my spade, I took the opportunity to ask him:

"What does your father write from Moscow, Seryozha?"

He shrugged his shoulders with assumed indifference.

"We don't correspond, Scribbler." (This nickname was given me because of my former profession.) "Granny wrote some time ago that he had been promoted."

"What did I tell you?" I exclaimed, delighted at the chance to speak on a theme close to my heart. "I knew he would go far. Believe me, Seryozha, I have an old and deep devotion to your father. I love this Emelyan Pugachev who turned into Suvorov —and the thunder of tanks on cobblestones, and the roar of loud-speakers and all the elaborate trumpery of our heroic age proudly proceeding across the face of the earth, clanking its medals. And if in spite of orders from above I failed to defend your father with my puny body, it was not for lack of will but of opportunity—the chance to save him just never occurred. It was he who was always saving others, he who prosecuted. Ah, if he were being stoned, how gladly would I have died for him! But he was not stoned."

My confidences did not seem to please Seryozha, for he changed the subject.

"Yes, well . . . My father considers me a

renegade. But my stepmother, Marina, she's quite different, and who would have believed it! I got a parcel from her yesterday."

"Oh, how like a Russian woman!" I exclaimed, my mouth watering. "Even as far back as the Decembrists . . . Princess Volkonsky and Princess Trubetskoy, following their husbands to Siberia! Do you remember Nekrasov's lines about Russian womanhood: 'She halts a bolting steed, she walks into a burning hut.' What is there in the parcel?"

"A box of liqueur chocolates."

"Nothing else?"

"Nothing."

It couldn't be helped. Liqueur chocolates were better than nothing. We gave half of them to our guard and, without climbing out of the ditch, made an exquisite picnic meal of the rest.

As always in moments of rest, we were entertained by Rabinovich. He had been acting rather oddly of late. Perhaps he had been driven out of his mind by the rehabilitation of the doctors. Rabinovich had been tried in connection with their case, but for some reason the authorities had forgotten to rehabilitate him. More probably, however, with his Jewish slyness, he was putting it on: the insane were treated leniently and quite often released into a madhouse.

Whatever the reason, his conversation had recently become so obscure as to be unintelligible.

He was always talking about God, history, and ends and means. Sometimes it was very funny.

Now, as he finished his last chocolate, he took out of his wadded jacket a curious piece of iron covered with earth and rust.

"How do you like that, Scribbler?" He turned to me with an inane smile.

Seryozha was delighted: "It's an archæological find: some unknown predecessor of Yermak must have passed through here, say in the sixteenth century. Perhaps he went right on to America. Perhaps he forestalled Columbus! The find should go to a museum at once and be kept under glass, in order to establish our priority."

The priority would certainly be established, I suggested, but as a lethal weapon the find must be handed in to the camp authorities.

It was a dagger, eaten away by rust and with a handle shaped like a crucifix.

"How do you like that?" asked Rabinovich again. "A nice place they found for God—the handle of a deadly weapon. Are you going to deny it? God was the end and they turned him into the means—a handle. And the dagger was the means and became the end. They changed places. Ay-ay-ay! And where are God and the dagger now? Among the eternal snows, both of them!"

"We've had quite enough of your survivals of the religious past!" I moved nervously away from

125

him. (Evidently Citizen Rabinovich had been sent here for good reason.) "Everyone knows that there is no God. We don't believe in God, we believe in dialectics."

Rabinovich leapt up, a puny Jew with a shorn head, in tattered, muddy trousers and with a rusty dagger under his arm.

"And what d'you think I'm saying? Am I arguing with you? Not on your life."

Seizing the dagger in both hands, he raised it like an umbrella and poked it at the sky which hung lowering over our ditch.

"In the name of God! With the help of God! In place of God! Against God!" He really did sound like a madman now. "And now there is no God, only dialectics. Forge a new dagger for the new Purpose at once!"

I was just about to object when the soldier who guarded us from the danger of escaping woke up on his hillock and shouted:

"You there, in the ditch! You've been wagging your tongues long enough. Get on with your work."

We took up our spades as one man.

ON SOCIALIST REALISM

Translated by George Dennis
Introduction by Czeslaw Milosz

On Socialist Realism is regarded as the theoretical companion and justification of the imaginative world presented in Abram Tertz's novel, *The Trial Begins*. It arrived simultaneously with the novel in the West and was first published by the French review *L'Esprit*. Two leading intellectual magazines in Europe, *Kultura* in Paris and *Il Tempo Presente* in Rome, subsequently published them together as complementary works. The work originally appeared in this country in the pages of *Dissent* magazine.

INTRODUCTION

The essay which follows was written in the Soviet Union and sent by its author through friends to Paris, asking that it be published. It came out first in 1959, in a French translation, in the Paris monthly **Esprit**. We need have no doubt as to its authenticity. We do not know the writer's name, nor would there be any point in trying to discover it. All the evidence goes to show, however, that he belongs to the younger generation of Russian writers, educated entirely under the postrevolutionary system. The fact that he has decided to have his work published abroad shows his belief in the importance of what he has to say. Let us consider this step: here we have a man with ample talent for attaining popularity in his own country, but who secretly writes something intended at best for reading by a small group of intimates. He then goes to a great deal of trouble to place his manuscript

131

in reliable keeping, and in this way it is brought across the frontiers. He knows full well the risk he runs should the authorities identify him as the author, while at the same time the preservation of his anonymity means that he can acquire neither fame nor money, even if his work is translated into many languages. At the same time he must also face the thorny problem of his loyalty as a citizen, for he lives in a state which forbids writers to publish without permission, and which regards violation of this rule as tantamount to violation of a citizen's duties, i.e., treason. This man has chosen to do what is condemned by the existing institutions and by the community formed by these institutions, for he sees no other way to voice his beliefs.

But American readers would be mistaken if they attributed their own values and perspectives to this anonymous Russian writer, and regarded him as a supporter of the Western way of life, for instance. Were this so, the situation would be relatively simple (an internal enemy of the system would have found means to reveal himself). If we are to understand him, we must abandon the division of people into Communists and anti-Communists. If this anonymous Russian were asked whether he is a Communist or an anti-Communist, he would almost certainly shrug and answer: "What does that

132

*mean?" Only one kind of reality exists for him: it
is that in which he has grown up and which forms
his daily environment. The world outside the Soviet
Union might just as well not exist, as far as he is
concerned. He lives with the problems of his own
community, and it is significant that he uses the
form "we"—"we did this and that," "we believed,"
"we ought to" . . . This essay should be taken as
a voice participating in an internal discussion
among Soviet writers; in conditions of greater freedom, his voice would be regarded as a manifestation
of the normal right to criticize.*

*To what extent does this anonymous Russian
express the trends prevailing in the society he belongs to? There is a good deal of evidence to show
that his views are shared by a large proportion of
the intellectuals, particularly among the younger
generation. The Russian press has published attempts to reach conclusions in a vein similar to
this essay, though they are cautious and half-
hearted. Where this anonymous Russian differs
from his fellow writers is in the boldness with
which he goes to the heart of the matter. Outside
the Soviet Union proper, in the countries of Eastern Europe now ruled by the Communists, his ideas
would cause no surprise. In some of these countries, where matters of the same kind are openly*

133

discussed, such arguments as we find in this essay are, at least unofficially, as plain as daylight to everyone.

Some Americans may believe that socialist realism, or "socrealism," as it is called, is nothing more than a style applied in the literature and art of the Soviet Union and in those areas to which its influence extends, a style which bears witness to the nineteenth-century tastes of bureaucrats for wedding-cake architecture, for flat colors in painting, and for plush luxury. That anyone who opposes this system of aesthetics is committing a political offense might appear fantastic. But unfortunately, socrealism is not merely a question of taste. It is a philosophy, too, and the cornerstone of official doctrine worked out in Stalin's days. Socrealism is directly responsible for the deaths of millions of men and women, for it is based on the glorification of the state by the writer and artist, whose task it is to portray the power of the state as the greatest good, and to scorn the sufferings of the individual. It is thus an effective anaesthetic. The inferiority of poetry, novels, plays, and pictures produced in accordance with this formula cannot be avoided, since reality, which is quite disagreeable, has to be passed over in silence in the name of an ideal, in the name of what ought to be. However, such an inferiority does not prevent, and indeed facilitates,

134

the extension of the influence of this kind of mass culture. The battle against socrealism is, therefore, a battle in defense of truth and consequently in defense of man himself.

Literature in Western Europe and America has never had the social character it possesses in Eastern Europe, except perhaps during the Reformation, when the writer spoke on behalf of a specific religious community. Although the political part played by certain writers has sometimes been great (Rousseau and Voltaire are obvious instances), the collective imagination has never had its archetype of bard, leader, and teacher. Historians of literature can refer only to the isolated example of Ireland in this respect. The violence of national and social conflicts in the eastern territories of Europe has made specific demands on writers. The origins of the Hungarian revolt in 1956 may well have been the Petöfi Club, so named after the nineteenth-century poet, and if so this has symbolic meaning and is simply the repetition of an older pattern. The history of Polish-Russian relations can largely be reduced to the collision of two different concepts of freedom, concepts maintained by writers and closely bound up with their pedagogic functions, different though these functions were in the two countries. After the 1917 Revolu-

tion in Russia, writers were given the honorary title of "Engineers of Souls." This was not particularly novel. It would never occur to the President of the United States to consider poems and plays, and to wonder whether their authors should be rewarded or exiled to Northern Alaska. But the authorities of America have never regarded literature as dangerous to themselves or as an important instrument for maintaining power. In Russia, on the other hand, Tsar Nicholas I personally censured Pushkin's verses. Revolutionary movements in Russia were created by the intelligentsia, who let off steam by writing and used words as a substitute for, or introduction to, action. When the Communist Party established its dictatorship, it retained the custom of allotting a high social rank to writers. And the theory of socrealism itself, which the Party adopted, took shape long before the Revolution, as this anonymous Russian shows. For these reasons the present work is not merely the reflection of arguments about aesthetics, of no interest to the public at large. The game is being played for much higher stakes.

Faced with statements such as those made by the anonymous Russian writer, issuing from the mysterious East, many Western readers may well tend to be incredulous. This irony, this kind of lyrical rage, strikes them as the privilege of modern writing, which could not have developed in a country deprived for decades of any kind of contact with the outside. Hence the suspicion may arise that here we have a case of the "internal émigré," imitating forbidden but longed-for foreign models. But to claim this would be to disregard the fact that Russian literature is vast enough to provide models to satisfy anyone. Even before 1917, Russia was one of the biggest consumers of books, and although most of the enormous number of books published in Russia since the Revolution are official and mediocre, there also have been a good many Russian or foreign "classics"—the last in excellent translations. This saturation by the printed word constantly creates, as it were, a surplus of demand, which cannot be satisfied by the current monotonous production. Even during the worst periods, a second current has always existed alongside the official one: the unpublished Boris Pasternak, for instance, had a few thousand admirers who knew his verses by heart. When "coexistence" started, tourists who visited Moscow brought back poems circulating in manuscript mainly among young people. These were examples of a large body of totally unknown works by prisoners in concentration camps and by students. Some are remarkable for their high quality, and all are imbued with various shades of sarcasm and irony. The anony-

mous Russian is therefore not alone in his stylistic leanings.

The problem of socrealism is much less simple than it might appear at first sight. Despite many attempts, the elements which constitute its theory have never been combined into a harmonious whole. In fiction, the division of characters into "good guys" and "bad guys" is required just as it is in any Western. The hero is allowed to have some doubts and make some mistakes, but good must finally triumph. Yet this good does not mean morality based on the Ten Commandments, but simply the individual's conformity with the communal aim. And this aim is the victory of the Revolution throughout the world. But since victory can be obtained only through a state led by the Party, the aim is everything which assists the Party to increase the state's industrial, military, and other strength. So the norms of individual behavior are to be found not within an individual, but are determined from without: the "subjective honesty" of a man who, motivated by moral impulses, might condemn the use of tanks in Budapest does not lessen his "objective guilt," for the independence of Hungary would be at variance with the interests of the Soviet Union and hence with the interests of the Revolution, i.e., of all mankind. Although this rea-

soning is crude, it is not difficult to perceive its origins in the German philosophy of history of the first half of the nineteenth century, which introduced the concept of historical development taking place independent of our wishes and desires. This philosophy fell on remarkably fertile soil in Tsarist Russia, because its solidified social structure faced the individual with obstacles whenever he tried to exert his own will; he therefore learned to make the system itself responsible, even for his own incompetence. In this way powerful habits of mind were formed, encouraging dreams of revolution to solve all the personal problems of men and women faced with the world; moral norms were transferred from the inner forum of the conscience to a providential historical process. This transfer was characteristic of the Russian progressive intelligentsia, and was noticed by Dostoevski, who wrote in his Diary of a Writer in 1873: "By making man dependent on every error in the social system, the science of environment reduces man to total loss of personality, to total release from all individual obligations and any kind of independence, it reduces him to the worst slavery imaginable." This shows that the apparently naïve formulas for novels and plays, laid down by the Party for writers to follow, were preceded in Russia by many decades of argument as to the relations between the individual and society.

139

What the anonymous Russian writer does for us is to let us for a time enter the skin of a Russian, into a circle inaccessible to anyone without the same background of experiences and rooted in another tradition. His wide knowledge of Russian literature both old and new shows we are dealing with a professional, whose answers to the fundamental questions are not merely academic, for his own progress and realization of himself as a writer depend on them. The most important point in his argument seems to me to be this: the Great Aim— the glory of Russia as sung in the eighteenth century by Derzhavin—was found again at the moment when Lenin seized power, when Russia was torn asunder by the revolutionary movement, after the doubts and searches of the nineteenth century. From this time on, Russia has been the chosen nation, a Welthistorische *nation, since it has chosen to be the instrument of a providential historical process leading "out of iron necessity" to Communism throughout the world. The hymns of praise that were sung in the past to the Russian state, assurances of the high vocation of the Russians and their superiority to other nations, were justified* ex post. *The light of the universal task (the salvation of man) has dawned upon Russia. Therefore, singing the praises of that future happiness which is to be the lot of all men, and this ceaseless ode in*

*praise of themselves (which is what Soviet litera-
ture is), amounts at the same time to an ode in
praise of tomorrow. Socrealism emerged from the
fusion of two creeds: belief in the mission of
the Russian nation and belief in the mission of
the (Russian) proletariat. The anonymous Russian
writer has had the courage to reject both these
creeds, for he believes that an aim attained by
methods such as have been used changes into its
very opposite: "So that prisons should vanish forever, we built new prisons. So that all frontiers
should fall, we surrounded ourselves with a Chinese Wall. So that work should become a rest and
a pleasure, we introduced forced labor. So that not
one drop of blood be shed any more, we killed and
killed and killed."*

*The Communists of several countries west of the
Soviet Union—first the Yugoslavs, then the Hun-
garians and the Poles—adopted the phrase "the
humanizing of Marxism," and many of them paid
a high price to oppose what they regarded as a
parody of Karl Marx's thought. Literature and art
played a leading part in these attempts to do away
with dogmas that were crushing man, and it is no
exaggeration to say that the breakdown of socrealism has opened the prison gates. Nevertheless
the "humanizing of Marxism" depends in the first*

instance on changes in the Soviet Union, for until they come about, attempts undertaken in other countries ruled by the Communists will continue to fail. That is why the voice of this anonymous Russian is so important, and it is interesting to consider how far it bears witness to a ripening of new tendencies directed against the heritage of the Stalinist era, and also what prospects these new tendencies have of emerging triumphant. Moderate optimism seems called for, since the number of factors working for or against are about equal.

Technical progress requiring a whole army of highly educated specialists, and the development of education both in high schools and in universities, are bringing conditions into being in which social sciences, literature, and art shackled by dogma clearly do not fit. The main argument used by Soviet "liberals" is the fact that readers and audiences are more intelligent than the product served up to them by the highly paid practitioners of socialist realism. A simplified picture of the world is not enough; the demands of these readers and audiences cannot be satisfied until the presentation of life in the Soviet Union is cleared of its numerous taboos. The falsity of novels, poems, and plays which sterilize reality is too self-evident. These readers and audiences want the truth, at least as savage as that of Khrushchev's 1956 report. And

142

this public, capable of thinking for itself, is going to increase. Thus the very fact that the Soviet Union is changing into a highly industrialized country supports the campaign carried on by those who share the views of our anonymous writer, even though they have to be more circumspect in the way they set about uttering them.

Still, we must not forget that the writer is a Russian, and is guilty of lèse-majesté in criticizing his own civilization. His fellow countrymen obtain plenty of nourishment every day for their national pride, and the government makes sure that this nourishment never runs short. Though they cannot eat the moon, it bears the emblem of the hammer and sickle. Collective glory is not something fictitious; it is very real, and has been acquired by ruthless indifference to human life. Socrealism has served for several decades as a drug exciting activity, and the effectiveness of hymns of praise has been proved. Should this tried and tested creed be jettisoned, and, instead of rejoicing at measurable results, should one turn to what is immeasurable — the happiness and unhappiness of man?

Attempts at drawing analogies between the Russia of the past and present-day Russia may well lead to errors. Nonetheless, it is likely that the Russians who want freedom and justice find themselves in conflict with most of their fellow countrymen, just as their predecessors did. This is what happens when criticism of things as they are seems to go against patriotism. Admittedly, Russia is no exception in this respect, and there are other societies in which the cult of raison d'état *was and is highly developed. Yet, the case of Peter Chaadaev, author of* The Philosophical Letters, *gives some indication of the strength of this cult inside Russia. When Chaadaev, in 1836, published one of these* Letters, *public opinion was so incensed that the Tsar did not even think it necessary to jail the unfortunate philosopher: obedient doctors diagnosed the originator of the uproar as a lunatic. But as we now know, Chaadaev's severe judgments regarding his own country were little short of prophetic. Thus he said: ". . . we are one of those nations which do not seem to be an integral part of the human race, but which exist only to give some great lesson to the world. The instruction which we are destined to give will certainly not be lost: but who knows the day when we will find ourselves a part of humanity, and how much misery we shall experience before the fulfillment of our destiny?"*

Alexander Herzen, too, was to find that even the most progressive circles supported him only as long as he did not question the frontiers of the Tsarist Empire, and Russia's right to dominate the territories she had conquered. Each one of us should beat his breast and ask himself whether he does not tend to modify attacks on his own native institutions, if these attacks are likely to expose him to the charge of subversion and assisting enemies from without. Russia has given the world many evangelically pure men and women, fearless in condemning evil, and fully aware that that which is to be rendered unto God is not the same as that which is to be rendered unto Caesar. The writer of this essay is one of their number. Yet a government has effective means at its disposal to prevent independence of mind; for no matter what may be the feelings of those it governs, they will be united whenever national pride is to be upheld. We can only cling to the hope that the day is nevertheless approaching when the Russians "will find themselves a part of humanity."

Czeslaw Milosz

What is socialist realism? What is the meaning of this strange and jarring phrase? Can there be a socialist, capitalist, Christian, or Mohammedan realism? Does this irrational concept have a natural existence? Perhaps it does not exist at all; perhaps it is only the nightmare of a terrified intellectual during the dark and magical night of Stalin's dictatorship? Perhaps a crude propaganda trick of Zhdanov's or a senile fancy of Gorki's? Is it fiction, myth, or propaganda?

Such questions, we are told, are often asked in the West. They are hotly debated in Poland. They are also current among us, where they arouse eager minds, tempting them into the heresies of doubt and criticism.

Meanwhile, the productions of socialist realism are measured in billions of printed sheets, kilometers of canvas and film, centuries of hours. A thou-

147

sand critics, theoreticians, art experts, pedagogues are beating their heads and straining their voices to justify, explain, and interpret its material existence and dialectical character. The head of the state himself, the First Secretary of the Central Committee, tears himself away from pressing economic tasks to pronounce some weighty words on the country's aesthetic problems.[1]

The most exact definition of socialist realism is given in a statute of the Union of Soviet Writers: "Socialist realism is the basic method of Soviet literature and literary criticism. It demands of the artist the truthful, historically concrete representation of reality in its revolutionary development. Moreover, the truthfulness and historical concreteness of the artistic representation of reality must be linked with the task of ideological transformation and education of workers in the spirit of socialism." (First All-Union Congress of Soviet Writers, 1934, p. 716.)

This innocent formula is the foundation on which the entire edifice of socialist realism was erected. It includes the link between socialist realism and the realism of the past, as well as its new

[1] This refers to Khrushchev's speeches to Soviet intellectuals, collected and published in 1957 under the title *For a Close Link Between Literature and Art and the Life of the People.*

148

and distinguishing quality. The link lies in the *truthfulness* of the representation; the difference, in the ability to seize the *revolutionary development* and to educate readers in accordance with that development, *in the spirit of socialism*. The old realists, or, as they are sometimes called, critical realists (because they criticized bourgeois society), men like Balzac, Tolstoi, and Chekhov, truthfully represented life as it is. But not having been instructed in the genius and teachings of Marx, they could not foresee the future victories of socialism, and they certainly did not know the real and concrete roads to these victories.

The socialist realist, armed with the doctrine of Marx and enriched by the experience of struggles and victories, is inspired by the vigilant attention of his friend and teacher, the Communist Party. While representing the present, he listens to the march of history and looks toward the future. He sees the "visible traits of Communism," invisible to the ordinary eye. His creative work is a step forward from the art of the past, the highest peak of the artistic development of mankind and the most realistic of realisms.

Such, in a few words, is the general scheme of our art. It is amazingly simple, yet sufficiently elastic to comprehend Gorki, Mayakovski, Fadeev, Aragon, Ehrenburg, and hundreds of others. But we

149

cannot understand this concept at all as long as we skim the surface of the dry formula and do not penetrate into its deep and hidden meaning.

The gist of this formula—"the truthful, historically concrete representation of reality in its revolutionary development"—is founded on the concept of Purpose with a capital P. The Purpose is an all-embracing ideal, toward which truthfully represented reality ascends in an undeviating revolutionary movement. To direct this movement toward its end and to help the reader approach it more closely by transforming his consciousness—this is the Purpose of socialist realism, the most purposeful art of our time.

The Purpose is Communism, known in its early stage as socialism. A poet not only writes poems but helps, in his own way, to build Communism; so, too, do sculptors, musicians, agronomists, engineers, laborers, policemen, and lawyers, as well as theaters, machines, newspapers, and guns.

Our art, like our culture and our society, is teleological through and through. It is subject to a higher destiny, from which it gains its title of nobility. In the final reckoning we live only to speed the coming of Communism.

A tendency toward purpose is part of human nature. I extend my hand to receive the coins. I go

150

to a movie to spend some time with a pretty girl. I write a novel to earn glory and the gratitude of posterity. Each of my conscious moves is purposeful.

Animals do not have such long-range intentions. They are moved by instincts. They bite to bite, and not for the purpose of biting. They don't think about tomorrow, wealth, God. They live without facing any complex problems. But man invariably wants what he has not got. This quality of our nature finds its outlet in a feverish activity. We transform nature into our own image and turn nature into an object. Aimless rivers become arteries of communication. Aimless trees become paper filled with destiny.

Our abstract thought is no less teleological. Man explores the world by attributing to it his own purposefulness. He asks: "What is the use of the sun?" and answers: "To give light and heat." The animism of primitive peoples is the first attempt to conquer senseless chaos by endowing it with many aims, and to animate the indifferent universe with a life useful to man.

Science has not freed us from the childish questions of "Why?" Behind the causal relations that it establishes we find the hidden and distorted purposefulness of natural phenomena. Science says:

151

"Man descends from the monkey" instead of saying: "The destiny of the monkey is to become man."

However man may have originated, his appearance and purpose are inseparable from God—that is, from the highest idea of purpose which is accessible to us, if not through our understanding, then through our wish that there should be such a purpose. This is the final purpose of all that is and of all that isn't, and is the infinite—and probably purposeless—Purpose in itself. For how could Purpose have purposes?

There are periods of history when the presence of Purpose is evident, when minor passions are absorbed in the striving for God and He openly calls mankind to Himself. Thus arose the culture of Christianity which seized the Purpose in what is, perhaps, its most inaccessible meaning. Then came the era of individualism which proclaimed the freedom of the individual as the Purpose and set about worshipping this purpose with the aid of the Renaissance, humanism, superman, democracy, Robespierre, service, and other forms of worship. And now we have entered the era of a new world-wide system—that of socialist purposefulness.

A blinding light pours from this summit of thought. "A world that we can imagine, more material and better suited to human needs than Christian paradise"—thus was Communism defined by the Soviet writer Leonid Leonov.

Words fail us when we try to talk about it. We choke with enthusiasm and we use mostly negative comparisons to describe the splendor that is waiting for us. Then, under Communism, there will be no rich and no poor, no money, wars, jails, frontiers, diseases—and maybe no death. Everybody will eat and work as much as he likes, and labor will bring joy instead of sorrow. As Lenin promised, we will make toilets of pure gold . . . But what am I talking about?

What words and what colors are needed
To describe these grandiose heights
Where whores are as modest as virgins
And hangmen as tender as mothers?

The modern mind cannot imagine anything more beautiful and splendid than the Communist ideal. The best that it can do is to restore to circulation old ideals of Christian love and the liberty of the individual. But it has been unable so far to set up a new Purpose.

Where socialism is concerned, the Western liberal individualist or Russian skeptical intellectual is about in the same position as the cultured and intelligent Roman with regard to victorious Christianity. He called the new faith of the crucified God

153

barbarous and naïve, laughed over the lunatics who worshipped the cross—that Roman guillotine—and believed that the doctrines of the Trinity, the Immaculate Conception, the Resurrection, etc., made no sense whatsoever. But it was quite above his powers to advance any serious arguments against the *ideal* of Christ as such. True, he could say that the best parts of the moral code of Christianity were borrowed from Plato, just as contemporary Christians assert here and there that Communism took its noble aims from the Gospel. But could he say that God conceived as Love or Goodness was evil or monstrous? And can we say that the universal happiness, promised for the Communist future, is evil?

For don't I know that blindfold thrusts
Will not make darkness yield to light?
Am I a monster? Is not the happiness of millions
Closer to me than empty luck for a few?

PASTERNAK

We are helpless before the enchanting beauty of Communism. We have not lived long enough to invent a new Purpose and to go beyond ourselves—into the distance that is beyond Communism.

It was the genius of Marx that he proved the earthly paradise, of which others had dreamed before him, was actually the Purpose which Fate destined for man. With the aid of Marx, Communism passed from moral efforts of isolated individuals— "Oh, where are you, golden age?"—into the sphere of universal history, which became purposeful as never before and turned into mankind's march toward Communism.

At once, everything fell into place. An iron necessity and a strict hierarchical order harnessed the flow of centuries. The ape stood up on its hind legs and began its triumphant procession toward Communism. The system of primitive Communism arose because it was fated to grow into slavery; slavery, to give birth to feudalism; feudalism, to capitalism; and finally capitalism, so that it could give way to Communism. That is all! The magnificent aim is achieved, the pyramid is crowned, history at an end.

A truly religious person relates all the splendid variety of life to his divinity. He cannot understand another faith. He believes in the Purpose so that he can despise other purposes. He shows the same fanaticism—or, if you prefer, *printsipialnost'*—with regard to history.[1] A consistent Christian views the entire history previous to the birth of

[1] *Printsipialnost'* is a Russian word with no English equivalent. It describes the mental habit of referring every matter, however small, concrete, or trivial, to lofty and abstract principles.

Christ as the prehistory of Christ. From the point of view of the monotheist, the pagans existed only to call upon themselves the will of the only God and, after a suitable preparation, to become monotheists.

It can therefore hardly surprise us that, in another religious system, ancient Rome has become an indispensable stage on the road to Communism. Or that the Crusades are explained not by their internal dynamics, by the ardent efforts of Christians, but by the action of the omnipresent forces of production that are now ensuring the collapse of capitalism and the triumph of socialism. True faith is not compatible with tolerance. Neither is it compatible with historicism, i.e., with tolerance applied to the past. And though the Marxists call themselves historical materialists, their historicism is actually reduced to a desire to regard life as a march toward Communism. Other movements are of little interest to them. Whether they are right or wrong is a matter of dispute. What is beyond dispute is that they are consistent.

If we ask a Westerner why the French Revolution was necessary, we will receive a great many different answers. One will reply that it happened to save France; another, that it took place to lead the nation into an abyss of moral experiments; a third, that it came to give to the world the great principles of Liberty, Equality, and Fraternity; a fourth, that the French Revolution was not necessary at all. But if you ask any Soviet schoolboy—to say nothing of the beneficiaries of our higher education—you will invariably receive the correct and exhaustive reply: the French Revolution was needed to clear the way to Communism.

The man who received a Marxist education knows the meaning of both past and future. He knows why this or that idea, event, emperor, or military leader was needed. It is a long time since men had such an exact knowledge of the meaning of the world's destiny—not since the Middle Ages, most likely. It is our great privilege to possess this knowledge once more.

The teleological nature of Marxism is most obvious in the works of its latest theorists. They brought to Marxism the clarity, strength, and rigor of military orders and economic decrees. A good example is Stalin's judgment on the role of ideas, taken from the fourth chapter of the *Short Course of History of the Communist Party of the Soviet Union:*

"There exist different ideas and theories. There are old ideas and theories which have outlived their time and serve the interests of outdated forces of society. Their significance lies in their hampering the growth of the society and its forward march.

There are also new, advanced ideas and theories which serve the interests of the advanced forces of society. Their significance lies in facilitating the growth of the society and its forward march."

As long as its famous author lived, the *Short Course* was the bedside book of every Soviet citizen. The entire literate population was constantly urged to study it and in particular its fourth chapter, containing the quintessence of the Marxist creed and written by Stalin himself. A quotation from V. Il'enkov's novel *The Great Highway* illustrates the universal validity that was attached to the *Short Course:*

"Father Degtyarev brought in a small volume and said: 'Everything is said here, in the fourth chapter.' Vinkentii Ivanovich took the book and thought: 'There is no book on this earth that contains everything that a man needs . . .' But Vinkentii Ivanovich [a typical skeptical intellectual] soon realized that he was wrong and accepted Degtyarev's view which was that of all advanced people: This book 'contains everything that a man needs.' "

Every word of this quotation is pervaded by the spirit of purposefulness. Even the ideas that do not favor the movement toward the Purpose have their destiny: to hamper the movement toward the Purpose (once, no doubt, the destiny of Satan). "Idea," "superstructure," "base," "law of nature," "econom-ics," "forces of production"—all these abstract and impersonal concepts suddenly come to life, are covered with flesh and blood and become like gods and heroes, angels and devils. They create purposes and suddenly, from the pages of philosophical trea-tises and scientific investigations, there resounds the voice of the great religious Mystery: "The base produces the superstructure so that it can serve the base." (J. Stalin: *Marxism and Linguistic Ques-tions.*)

This is not the only happy turn of phrase of Stalin's which the author of the Bible might envy. The specific teleology of Marxist thought consists in leading *all* concepts and objects to the Purpose, referring them all to the Purpose, and defining them all through the Purpose. The history of all epochs and nations is but the history of humanity's march toward Communism, and the history of the world's thought happened, so to say, in order to bring forth "scientific materialism," i.e. Marxism, i.e. the Phi-losophy of Communism. The history of philosophy, proclaimed Zhdanov, "is the history of the birth, rise and development of the scientific world view and its laws. As materialism grew and developed in the struggle against idealism, so the history of philosophy is the history of the struggle between materialism and idealism." (A. A. Zhdanov, "Con-

159

tribution to the Discussion of G. F. Aleksandrov's *History of Western European Philosophy,*" June 24, 1947.) These proud words seem like the voice of God Himself exclaiming: "The whole of history is My history, and since I assert myself in the struggle with Satan, world history is also the history of My struggle with Satan."

And so it rises before us, the sole Purpose of all Creation, as splendid as eternal life and as compulsory as death. And we fling ourselves toward it, breaking all barriers and rejecting anything that might hamper our frantic course. We free ourselves without regret from belief in an afterlife, from love of our neighbor, from freedom of the individual and other prejudices, by now rather shopworn and looking all the sorrier by comparison with the great Ideal before us. Thousands of martyrs of the Revolution gave up their lives for the new religion and surpassed the first Christians in their sufferings, their steadfastness, and their holiness:

> *Polish commanders*
> *Branded our backs with*
> *Five-pointed stars.*
> *Mamontov's bands*
> *Buried us alive*
> *Up to our necks.*
> *The Japanese*

160

Burned us in the fireboxes
of locomotives
And poured lead and tin
Into our mouths.
They all roared:
"Abjure!"
But from our burning throats
Only three words came:
"Long
Live
Communism!"

MAYAKOVSKI

To our new God we sacrificed not only our lives, our blood, and our bodies. We also sacrificed our snow-white soul, after staining it with all the filth of the world.

It is fine to be gentle, to drink tea with preserves, to plant flowers and cultivate love, nonresistance to evil, and other philanthropies. But whom did they save and what did they change in this world, these ancient virgins of both sexes, these egoists of humanism who bought themselves an easy conscience penny by penny and rented themselves a cozy corner in the heavenly almshouses?

We did not want salvation for ourselves but for all of humanity. Instead of sentimental sighs, individual perfection, and amateur dramatics for the

161

benefit of the hungry, we set about to correct the universe according to the best of models, the shining model of the Purpose which we approached ever more closely.

So that prisons should vanish forever, we built new prisons. So that all frontiers should fall, we surrounded ourselves with a Chinese Wall. So that work should become a rest and a pleasure, we introduced forced labor. So that not one drop of blood be shed any more, we killed and killed and killed.

In the name of the Purpose we turned to the means that our enemies used: we glorified Imperial Russia, we wrote lies in *Pravda* [Truth], we set a new Tsar on the now empty throne, we introduced officers' epaulettes and tortures. . . . Sometimes we felt that only one final sacrifice was needed for the triumph of Communism—the renunciation of Communism.

O Lord, O Lord—pardon us our sins!

Finally, it was created, our world, in the image and likeness of God. It is not yet Communism, but it is already quite close to Communism. And so we rise, stagger with weariness, encircle the earth with bloodshot eyes, and do not find around us what we hoped to find.

Why do you laugh, scum? Why do you claw with your well-cared-for nails the spots of blood and dirt that have stuck to our jackets and uniforms? You say that this is not Communism, that we took the wrong turning and that we are further from Communism now than when we started. Well then, where is *your* Kingdom of God? Show it! Where is the free personality of the superman that you promised?

Achievements are never identical with the original aim. The means used to reach the aim change its original appearance into something unrecognizable. The stakes of the Inquisition helped to establish the Gospel; but what is left of the Gospel after the stakes have done their work? Yet all of them—the stakes of the Inquisition and the Gospel, the Massacre of St. Bartholomew and St. Bartholomew himself—add up to one great Christian culture.

Yes, we live in Communism. It resembles our aspirations about as much as the Middle Ages resembled Christ, modern Western man resembles the free superman, and man resembles God. But all the same, there is *some resemblance,* isn't there?

This resemblance lies in the subordination of all our actions, thoughts, and longings to that sole Purpose which may have long ago become a meaningless word but still has a hypnotic effect on us and pushes us onward and onward—we don't know where. And, obviously, art and literature could not but get caught in the meshes of that system and

163

become, as Lenin predicted, "a small wheel and a small screw" of the gigantic state machine. "Our magazines, both scientific and artistic, cannot be apolitical . . . The strength of Soviet literature, the most advanced in the world, is that it is a literature for which there can be no other interests than those of the people and of the state. (Decree of the Central Committee of the CPSU [b], August 14, 1946.)

It must be remembered, when reading this decree of the Central Committee, that the interests of the people and of the state—which, incidentally, are exactly the same from the point of view of the state—have but a single aim: the all-pervading and all-absorbing Communism. "Literature and art are part of the whole people's struggle for Communism. . . . The highest social destiny of art and literature is to mobilize the people to the struggle for new advances in the building of Communism." (N. S. Khrushchev, "For a Close Link Between Literature and Art and the Life of the People," *Kommunist* magazine, number 12, 1957.)

When Western writers deplore our lack of freedom of speech, their starting point is their belief in the freedom of the individual. This is the foundation of their culture, but it is organically alien to Communism. A true Soviet writer, a true Marxist, will not accept these reproaches, and will not even know what they are all about. What freedom—if the comparison be permitted—does the religious person require from God? The freedom to praise God still more ardently?

Contemporary Christians, who have broken their spiritual fast and accepted the spirit of individualism, with its free elections, free enterprise, and free press, occasionally abuse the phrase "freedom of choice" that Christ is supposed to have bequeathed us. This sounds like a dubious borrowing from the parliamentary system to which they are accustomed, for it bears no resemblance to the Kingdom of God, if only because no president or prime minister is ever elected in paradise. Even the most liberal God offers only one freedom of choice: to believe or not to believe, to be for Him or for Satan, to go to paradise or to hell. Communism offers just about the same right. If you don't want to believe, you can go to jail—which is by no means worse than hell. And for the man who believes, for the Soviet writer to whom Communism is the purpose of his own and humanity's existence (and otherwise there is no place for him either in our literature or in our society), there can be no such dilemma. For the man who believes in Communism, as Khrushchev correctly noted in one of his latest cultural pronouncements, "for the artist who truly wants to serve his people, the question does not arise of whether he is free or not in his creative work. For him, the question of which approach to the phenomena of reality to choose is clear. He need not conform or force himself; the true representation of life from the point of view of Communist *partiinost'*[1] is a necessity of his soul. He holds firmly to these positions, and affirms and defends them in his work."

It is with the same joyous facility that this artist accepts the directives of the Party and the government, from the Central Committee and its First Secretary. For who, if not the Party and its leader, knows best what kind of art we need? It is, after all, the Party that leads us to the Purpose in accordance with all the rules of Marxism-Leninism, the Party that lives and works in constant contact with God. And so we have in it and in its leader the wisest and most experienced guide, who is competent in all questions of industry, linguistics, music, philosophy, painting, biology, etc. He is our Commander, our Ruler, our High Priest. To doubt his word is as sinful as to doubt the will of God.

These are the aesthetic and psychological concepts the knowledge of which is indispensable to anyone who would penetrate the secret of socialist realism.

[1] *Partiinost'* is the point of view that considers everything in terms of the correct Party line.

PART TWO

Works produced by socialist realists vary in style and content. But in all of them the Purpose is present, whether directly or indirectly, open or veiled. They arc panegyrics on Communism, satires on some of its many enemies, or descriptions of life "in its revolutionary development," i.e., life moving toward Communism.

Having chosen his subject, the Soviet writer views it from a definite angle. He wants to discover what potentialities it contains that point to the splendid Purpose. Most subjects of Soviet literature have in common a remarkable purposefulness. They all develop in one direction, and a direction well known in advance. This direction may exhibit variations in accordance with time, place, conditions, etc., but it is invariable in its course and its destiny: to remind the reader once more of the triumph of Communism.

167

Each work of socialist realism, even before it appears, is thus assured of a happy ending. The ending may be sad for the hero, who runs every possible risk in his fight for Communism; but it is happy from the point of view of the superior Purpose; and the author never neglects to proclaim his firm belief in our final victory, either directly or through a speech of his dying hero. Lost illusions, broken hopes, unfulfilled dreams, so characteristic of literature of other eras and systems, are contrary to socialist realism. Even when it produces a tragedy, it is an *Optimistic Tragedy*, the title of Vishnevski's play in which the heroine dies at the end but Communism triumphs.

A comparison between some representative titles of Soviet and Western literature is revealing. *Journey to the End of the Night* (Céline); *Death in the Afternoon* and *For Whom the Bell Tolls* (Hemingway); *Everyone Dies Alone* (Fallada); *A Time to Live and a Time to Die* (Remarque); *Death of a Hero* (Aldington) are all in minor key. *Happiness* (Pavlenko); *First Joys* (Fedin); *It is Well!* (Mayakovski); *Fulfilled Wishes* (Kaverin); *Light over the Earth* (Babaevski); *The Victors* (Bagritski); *The Victor* (Simonov); *The Victor* (Chirikov); *Spring in the Victory Collective Farm* (Gribachev), and so on, are all in a major key.

The splendid aim toward which the action develops is sometimes presented directly at the end of the work. This method was brilliantly used by Mayakovski. All his major works after the Revolution end with passages about Communism or with fantastic scenes describing life in the future Communist state (*Mystery Bouffe; 150,000,000; About This; Vladimir Il'ich Lenin; It is Well!; With a Full Voice*). Gorki, who during the Soviet era wrote mainly about the days before the Revolution, ended most of his novels and plays—*The Artamonov Affair; The Life of Klim Samgin; Egor Bulichev; Dostigaev*—with a vision of the victorious Revolution, which was a stage on the way to Communism, and the concluding gesture of the old world.

Even when the book does not end with such a grandiose denouement, it still exists implicitly and symbolically, commanding the development of characters and events. For example, many of our novels and stories deal with the work of a factory, the building of a power plant, the application of an agricultural decree, and so on. An economic task is carried out in the course of the action (e g., the start of building introduces the plot; the end of building, the denouement). But the task is presented as an indispensable stage on the way toward a higher purpose. In such a purposeful view, even technical processes acquire dramatic tension and can be followed with great interest. The reader finds out step by step how, against all kinds of obstacles, the plant was put to work, the "Victory" collective farm gathered a good crop of corn, and so on. He closes the book with a sigh of relief and realizes that we have made yet another step toward Communism.

Since Communism is for us the inescapable outcome of the historical process, many of our novels have made the impetuous course of time the mainspring of their action. The course of time, working its way toward the Purpose, works for us. The Soviet writer does not think in Proustian terms. He does not search for lost time; his motto is rather: "Time, march on!" He hastens the course of life and affirms that each day lived is not a loss but a gain for man—because it brings him closer to the desired ideal, even if only by one millimeter.

This purposefulness of the historic processes is linked with the great interest our writers show in history, both recent and remote. Recent historical events like the Civil War and collectivization are landmarks on the road we chose. In more remote eras it is, alas, harder to find the movement toward Communism. But if the writer concentrates hard enough he will uncover, even in the most remote of times, some phenomenon that might be called progressive because, in the final account, it aided in some way our victories of today. The writers merely anticipate somewhat and give these events the Purpose that they did not yet have. And so the leaders of the past like Ivan the Terrible, Peter the Great, or the peasant rebel Stenka Razin, though they did not know the word "Communism," still know quite well that our future will be brilliant. They never cease to celebrate this future from the pages of our historical novels, and they constantly gladden the heart of their readers by their astounding perspicacity.

Another subject is offered to our literature by the internal world of man's psychological life. This internal world moves toward the Purpose by dynamics of its own, fights against "the traces of the bourgeois past in its conscience," and re-educates itself under the influence of the Party and of surrounding life. A large part of Soviet literature is an "educational novel" which shows the Communist metamorphosis of individuals and entire communities. Many of our books turn around the representation of these moral and psychological processes, which aim at producing the Ideal man of the future. One such is Gorki's *Mother,* where an ignorant woman, defeated by life, is transformed into a conscious revolutionary. Written in 1906, this book is generally considered the first example of socialist realism. Or there is Makarenko's *Pedagogical Poem* about the young criminals who take the road to

171

honest work, or Ostrovski's novel *How the Steel Was Tempered*, i.e., how the steel of our youth was tempered in the fire of the Civil War and the cold of early Communist construction.

As soon as the literary character becomes fully purposeful and conscious of his purposefulness, he can enter that privileged caste which is universally respected and called "positive heroes." This is the Holy of Holies of socialist realism, its cornerstone and main achievement.

The positive hero is not simply a good man. He is a hero illuminated by the light of the most ideal of all ideals. Leonid Leonov called his positive hero "a peak of humanity from whose height the future can be seen." He has either no faults at all or else but a few of them—for example, he sometimes loses his temper a little. These faults have a twofold function. They help the hero to preserve a certain likeness to real men, and they provide something to overcome as he raises himself ever higher and higher on the ladder of political morality. However, these faults must be slight or else they would run counter to his basic qualities. It is not easy to enumerate these basic qualities of the positive hero: ideological conviction, courage, intelligence, will power, patriotism, respect for women, self-sacrifice, etc., etc. The most important, of course, are the clarity and directness with which he sees the Purpose and strives toward it. Hence the amazing precision of all his actions, thoughts, tastes, feelings, and judgments. He firmly knows what is right and what is wrong; he says plainly "yes" or "no" and does not confuse black with white. For him there are no inner doubts and hesitations, no unanswerable questions, and no impenetrable secrets. Faced with the most complex of tasks, he easily finds the solution—by taking the shortest and most direct route to the Purpose.

The positive hero first appeared in some books of Gorki's written in the first decade of the twentieth century. He started by proclaiming to the world: "One must say firmly yes or no!" Many were shocked by the self-assurance and straightforwardness of his formulations, by his tendency to preach at everyone around him, and by his pompous monologues celebrating his own virtues. Chekhov, when he managed to read through *The Petty Bourgeois,* frowned with embarrassment and advised Gorki to soften the loud proclamations of his hero. Chekhov feared pretentiousness worse than fire: he viewed such purple passages as a boastfulness foreign to the Russian character.

But Gorki was deaf to such advice. He did not fear the reproaches and sneers of the shocked intelligentsia and its repeated assertions that the new hero was dull-witted and narrow-minded. He knew that his hero was the man of the future and that "only men who are as pitiless, straight, and hard as swords will cut their way through." (*The Petty Bourgeois*, 1901.)

Since then the positive hero has gone through many changes and presented himself in many guises. He unrolled his positive qualities in many ways, grew big and sturdy, and finally drew himself up to his full stature. This happened as early as the 1930s, when the Soviet writers dropped their little cliques and their literary tendencies, and accepted, almost unanimously, the best and most advanced trend of all: socialist realism.

To read the books of the last twenty or thirty years is to feel the great power of the positive hero. First he spread in every direction, until he filled all our literature. There are books in which *all* the heroes are positive. This is but natural, since we are coming ever closer to the Purpose. So that if a book about the present deals not with the fight against the enemies but with, say, a model collective farm, then all its characters can and must be positive. To put negative characters in such a situation would, to say the least, be strange. And so we get dramas and novels where all moves smoothly and peacefully. If there is a conflict between the heroes, it is a conflict between good and better, model and supermodel. When these books appeared, their authors—men like Babaevski, Surkov, Sofronov, Virta, Gribachev, etc.—were highly praised and set up as examples for others. True, since the Twentieth Congress—one hardly knows why—our attitude toward them has changed somewhat and we apply to them the contemptuous adjective "conflictless." Once Khrushchev came out in defense of these writers, such reproaches were stilled somewhat, but they are still voiced here and there by intellectuals. They are unjust.

Since we don't want to lose face before the West, we occasionally cease to be consistent and declare that our society is rich in individualities and embraces many interests; and that it has differences of opinion, conflicts, and contradictions, and that literature is supposed to reflect all that.

True, we differ from each other in age, sex, nationality, and even intelligence. But whoever follows the Party line knows that these are heterogeneities within a homogeneity, differences of opinion within a single opinion, conflicts within a basic absence of conflict. We have one aim—Communism; one philosophy—Marxism; one art—socialist realism. This was well put by a Soviet writer of no great literary gifts but politically irreproachable: "Russia took its own road—that of unanimity. . . . For thousands of years men suffered from differences of opinion. But now we, Soviet men and women, for the first time agree with each other, talk one language that we all understand, and think identically about the main things in life. It is this unanimity that makes us strong and superior to all other people in the world, who are internally torn and socially isolated through their differences of opinion." (V. Il'enkov, *The Great Highway*, a novel which appeared in 1949 and was awarded the Stalin Prize.)[1]

Beautifully put! Yes, we really are all alike and we are not ashamed of it. Those of us who suffer from superfluous differences of thought we punish severely by excluding them from life and literature. There can be no substantial differences of opinion in a country where even the anti-Party elements confess their errors and wish to rectify them as soon as possible, and incorrigible enemies of the people ask to be shot. Still less can there be such differences among honest Soviet people and least of all among positive heroes who think only of spreading their virtues all over the world and of re-educating the few remaining dissidents into unanimity.

[1] One cannot but recall in this connection Khrushchev's *cri de coeur* against the Jews: "They are all individualists and all intellectuals. They want to talk about everything, they want to discuss everything, they want to debate everything—and they come to totally different conclusions!"

True, there are still disagreements between the vanguard and the backward, and there is still the sharp conflict with the capitalist world that does not let us sleep in peace. But we do not doubt for a single moment that all these contradictions will be resolved, that the world will become unified and Communist, and that the last, by competing with each other, shall become the first. This great harmony is the final Purpose of Creation, this beautiful absence of conflict is the future of socialist realism. And so we can hardly reproach those overharmonious writers who have indeed withdrawn from contemporary conflicts but only to glance at the future, i.e., to find out how they can best pay the debt which, as writers, they owe to socialist realism. Babaevski and Surkov have not deviated from the sacred principles of our art, but have rather developed it logically and organically. They embody the higher stage of socialist realism and the embryo of the coming Communist realism.

The growing strength of the positive hero is shown not only in his incredible multiplication—he has far surpassed other kinds of literary character in quantity, put them into the shade, and sometimes replaced them altogether. His qualitative growth has also been remarkable. As he approaches the Purpose, he becomes ever more positive, great, and splendid. He also becomes more and more per-

177

suaded of his own dignity, especially when he compares himself to contemporary Western man and realizes his immeasurable superiority. "But our Soviet man has left *them* far behind. He is now close to the peak while they are still wandering in the foothills"—this is the way simple peasants talk in our novels. And the poet runs out of words when he tries to describe this superiority, this incomparable positiveness of our positive hero:

> *Nobody rose so high*
> *For centuries and centuries.*
> *You are above all glory,*
> *You are beyond all praise.*

M. ISAKOVSKI

The novel *Russian Forest* by Leonid Leonov, the first writer to be awarded a Lenin Prize—which replaced the Stalin Prize—is the best work of socialist realism for the last five years or so. It contains a remarkable scene. The brave girl Polya, entrusted with a dangerous mission, makes her way to the rear of the enemy—the action takes place during the Patriotic War. As a camouflage she is supposed to collaborate with the Germans. She plays this part for a while in talking to a Nazi officer, but with great difficulty: it is morally painful to her to talk the enemy's language. Finally she cannot stand it any more and reveals her true self and her superiority to the German officer: "I am a girl of my time . . . maybe just an ordinary girl, but I am the world's tomorrow . . . and you should stand up, yes, stand up when you talk to me, if you have a trace of self-respect left! But there you sit, only because you are nothing but a horse that the Chief Hangman puts through its paces . . . Well, don't just sit there, do something! . . . Get up and show me the place where Soviet girls are shot!"

The fact that by this pompous tirade Polya betrays herself and moreover harms the mission with which she has been entrusted does not disturb the author in the least. He finds an easy way out of the resulting situation. The noble purity of Polya's heart converts a *starosta*[1] who happened to listen to the conversation. His conscience suddenly awakens, he shoots at the German, loses his life, and saves Polya's.

But this is not what matters. It does not matter so much that the *starosta* moved, within the batting of an eyelid, from the rearguard to the vanguard. What matters very much more is that we have here the straight and immutable determination of the positive hero raised, we might say, to the second

[1] A peasant official put in charge of the village by the Germans.

power. Polya's behavior may seem stupid from the point of view of common sense. But it is filled with an immense religious and aesthetic significance. Under no circumstances, even to further his task, does the positive hero dare so much as to look negative. Even in the face of the enemy who must be outwitted and cheated, he must demonstrate his positive qualities. They cannot be hidden or camouflaged: they are written on his brow and they sound in his every word. And so he defeats the enemy not by cleverness, wits, or physical strength but by his proud attitude alone.

Polya's deed is the key to much that to the nonbeliever appears grossly exaggerated, stupid, and false—especially the positive hero's propensity to pontificate on elevated themes. He makes Communist assertions at home and at work, in friends' homes and on lonely walks, on the love couch and on the deathbed. But this is not a contradiction; positive heroes were created to present to the world, on every suitable and unsuitable occasion, models of purposefulness:

> *Measure*
> *Each detail*
> *By the great*
> *Purpose*
>
> **MAYAKOVSKI**

Only men who are as pitiless, straight, and
hard as swords will cut their way through.

GORKI

Never before have there been heroes like this.
Though Soviet writers are proud of the great traditions of nineteenth-century Russian literature,
which they want to follow in every possible way
and sometimes actually do follow (even though
they constantly upbraid Western writers for slav-
ishly imitating outworn literary canons), the positive hero of socialist realism is a break with the
tradition, not its continuation.

A very different type of hero prevailed in the
last century, and Russian culture lived and thought
differently then. Compared with the fanatical re-
ligiosity of our time, the nineteenth century seems
atheist, tolerant, disoriented. It was soft and shriv-
elled, feminine and melancholy, full of doubts,
inner contradictions, and pangs of conscience.
Chernyshevski and Pobedonostsev, the great radical and the great reactionary, were perhaps the
only two men of the century who really believed
in God. Of course, an incalculable number of peasants and old women also believed in God; but they
were not the makers of history and culture. Culture
was made by a handful of mournful skeptics who
thirsted for God simply because they had no God.

181

But you might object: How about Tolstoi and Dostoevski, how about the thousands of other "seekers after God," from the Populists to Merezhkovski, whose search for God has lasted well into the middle of *our* century? I assume that to search means not to have. He who has, who really believes, does not search. And what should he search for, if everything is clear and all that he has to do is to *follow* God? God is not found; He finds us and comes upon us. When He has found us, we cease to search and start to act, doing His will.

The nineteenth century was a century of searching, of ardent or calm aspirations, unwilling or unable to find a solid place under the sun, torn by uncertainties and dualism. Dostoevski regretted that the Russian was so broad—he should be narrowed, he felt. But Dostoevski was so broad himself that he could embrace within himself both Orthodoxy and nihilism. He could find room in his soul for all the Karamazovs—Alyosha, Mitya, Ivan, Fedor (some would add Smerdyakov). We don't know to this day which of them predominated. For breadth excludes faith: no wonder we narrowed ourselves down to Marxism, thus fulfilling Dostoevski's wish. Dostoevski fully understood the temptations of breadth, eternally disputed with himself, and passionately wished to end these disputes, offensive to the one God.

This thirst for God, this wish to believe, arose—as did the search—in a spiritual desert. It was not yet faith, and if the wish preceded faith—Blessed are they who thirst!—it is like hunger preceding a meal. Though a hungry man is ready to eat, there is not always a meal waiting for him. The great hunger of the nineteenth century perhaps conditioned us Russians to throw ourselves so greedily upon the food prepared by Marx and to devour it even before we had time to analyze its taste, smell, and consequences. But this hundred years' hunger was itself caused by the catastrophic absence of food: it was a hunger of godlessness. That is why it proved so exhausting and felt so unbearable, making us "go among the people," turn radical and renegade, and suddenly remember that we are, after all, Christians. . . . But there was no relief anywhere:

> I want to make peace with heaven,
> I want to love, I want to pray,
> I want to believe in the good.

But who is it that cries so anxiously for faith? None other than the Demon of Lermontov's poem.[1] It is the very "spirit" of doubt that has torn us so

[1] Lermontov, the great romantic poet, wrote *The Demon* in 1842.—Tr.

long and so painfully. He confirms that it is not the saints who thirst for God but those who have no God and have left Him.

It is a very Russian Demon. He is too inconsistent in his passion for evil to figure as a full Devil and too inconsistent in his repentance to make his peace with God and rejoin the obedient angels. His tone is not straightforward but ambiguous— "not day and not night, not light and not dark." There are only semi-tones, the secret glitter of twilight that was later glimpsed by the symbolist poet Blok and the symbolist painter Vrubel.

A consistent atheism, an extreme and inflexible denial of God, resembles religion more than this vague incertitude. For this is the crux of the Demon's problem: he has no faith and he suffers from lack of faith. His is the eternal motion upward and downward, backward and forward, between heaven and hell.

Remember what happened to the Demon? He fell in love with Tamara, that divine beauty incarnated in a ravishing woman, and decided to believe in God. But as soon as he kissed Tamara she died, killed by his touch. She was taken from him, and he was once more alone in his anguished unbelief.

For a century this was also the story of Russian culture, which had been possessed by the Demon even before Lermontov. Russia went into a frenzied search for an ideal; and no sooner did she touch heaven than she fell. The slightest contact with God led to denying Him, and with the denial came the anguish of unrealized faith.

The universal genius of Pushkin took note of this collision in *The Prisoner of the Caucasus* and other early poems; but it was only in *Eugene Onegin* that he unfolded the theme in its full amplitude. The plot of *Onegin* is a simple anecdote: as long as Tatiana loves Onegin and is willing to belong to him, he is indifferent to her; but when she marries another, he falls in love with her passionately and hopelessly. Embedded in this banal story are contradictions on which Russian literature has dwelled to the days of Chekhov and Blok: contradictions of a spirit without God and of a Purpose irrevocably lost.

The central hero of this literature—Onegin, Pechorin of Lermontov's *Hero of Our Time*, Beltov of Herzen's *Whose Fault?*, Lavretski of Turgenev's *Nest of Gentlefolk* and Rudin of his novel of that name—is usually called "the superfluous man." For all his generous impulses he is unable to find a destiny and he presents a lamentable example of a purposelessness that is of no use to anybody. He is, as a rule, a reflective character, with tendencies to self-analysis and self-flagellation. His life is full of unrealized projects, and his fate is sad and

185

slightly ridiculous. A woman usually plays a fatal part in it.

Russian literature is full of love stories in which an inadequate man and a beautiful woman meet and part without achieving anything. The fault, of course, lies with the man, who does not know how to love his lady as she deserves, actively and with a purpose. Instead, he yawns with boredom, like Onegin and Rudin, or else he kills his beloved, like Aleko in Pushkin's *Gypsies* or Arbenin in Lermontov's *Masquerade*.

If only the hero were at least a low fellow, incapable of higher feelings! But no, he is a noble creature and the most attractive woman boldly offers him her heart and hand. But instead of rejoicing and taking life with a song, he commits some irresponsible acts and, against his own desires, does everything he can to ensure that his beloved shall not become his.

Judging by the literature of the time, all hearts were broken in nineteenth-century Russia and no children were born for a while. But the writers were not describing the actual life and customs of the Russian nobility; they were engaged in depth metaphysics of an aimlessly agitated spirit. In this literature, woman is the touchstone of man. His relations with her bare his weakness and, compromised by her strength and beauty, he descends

186

from the stage on which a heroic action was to be played, bows to fate, and sneaks out into nothingness with the shameful cry of a base, useless, superfluous man.

The women, those innumerable Tatianas, Lisas, Natalias, Bellas, and Ninas [Tatiana is the heroine of *Eugene Onegin;* Lisa of *A Nest of Gentlefolk;* Bella of *A Hero of Our Time*], shine like an ideal, chaste and beyond the reach of Onegins and Pechorins, who love them so clumsily and unsuccessfully. For Russian literature they served as a synonym of the ideal, as symbol of a higher Purpose.

For woman is generally considered a beautiful, pure, and nebulous creature. Not too much is asked of her: she need not be concrete and definite to save man; it is enough that she be pure and beautiful. And since she occupies, like every Purpose, a passive and waiting position, her beautiful, magical, mysterious, and not too concrete nature permits her to represent a higher stage of the ideal and to serve as a substitute for the absent and desired Purpose.

This was the woman that the nineteenth century found most to its liking. She impressed it by her vagueness, her mysteriousness, and her tenderness. Pushkin's dreamy Tatiana opened up an age; the "Beautiful Lady" to whom Blok dedicated his first

187

collected poems closed it. Tatiana was indispensable for Onegin to suffer *through the absence of somebody*. And, concluding a love story that lasted for a century, Blok took the Beautiful Lady as his Bride, only to betray Her and to lose Her and to torment himself all his life by the purposelessness of his existence.

Blok's poem *The Twelve*—a work at the boundary between two hostile and mutually exclusive cultures—contains an episode that puts a full stop to the love theme of the nineteenth century. The Red Guard Petka kills, against his will and in a fit of anger, his sweetheart, the prostitute Katka. The tragic murder and the sorrows of lost love resuscitate the old drama, known to us from the days of Lermontov's *Masquerade* and *Demon*. Blok himself used it in many variations—did not the fool Petka and big-mouthed Katka, with her new boy friend Harlequin-Vanka, issue from Blok's own Pierrot and Columbine? But if the old heroes, the Demons and Arbenins, just turn their emptied souls inside out and freeze into a hopeless sorrow, Petka, who followed in their footsteps, is not allowed to do it. His more politically conscious comrades rouse him and re-educate him:

> *You sure go on and on, you bastard,*
> *What are you? A little girl?*

> *Sure, you want to turn your soul*
> *Inside out for us to see? O.K.*
> *Come on, snap out of it, look smart,*
> *Get yourself under control!*
>
> *. . . . .*
>
> *And Petrukha soon slowed down*
> *His hurried steps*
>
> *. . . . .*
>
> *He threw back his head*
> *And became gay once more.*

Thus was born a new hero, never seen before. In bloody battles against the enemy—"I will drink blood for my black-browed beauty!"—and in the works and pains of the new era—"This is no time for babying!"—he cures himself of sterile reflections and useless pangs of conscience. He lifts his head proudly, cheers himself up, and enters Soviet literature under the flag of the new God whom Blok, from old habit, calls Jesus Christ:

> *Forward, forward,*
> *Working people!*

The superfluous man of the nineteenth century became even more superfluous in the twentieth. To the positive hero of the new era he was strange and incomprehensible. The superfluous man seemed to him much more dangerous than the openly nega-

189

tive enemy. After all, the enemy was like the positive hero—clear, straightforward, and, in his own way, purposeful. Only his significance was negative —to hinder the movement to the Purpose. But the superfluous man was a creature of different psychological dimensions, inaccessible to computation and regimentation. He is neither for the Purpose nor against the Purpose—he is outside the Purpose. Now this simply cannot be; it is a fiction, a blasphemy. While the whole world, having defined itself with regard to the Purpose, is divided into two antagonistic camps, he feigns not to understand this and keeps mingling his colors in vague and ambiguous schemes. He proclaims that there are no Reds and no Whites but simply people, poor, unfortunate, superfluous people:

> *They all lie in a row—*
> *No line between them.*
> *Look: soldiers!*
> *Who's ours? Who's theirs?*
> *He was white and now he's red—*
> *The blood reddened him.*
> *He was red and now he's white—*
> *Death whitened him.*

M. TSVETAEVA[1]

[1] Marina Tsvetaeva returned to Russia in 1940 after a long exile and committed suicide two years later. She has

In the religious struggle, the superfluous man proclaimed his neutrality and expressed his sympathy with both parties, as in these verses of the symbolist poet Voloshin:

> Both here and there, among the ranks
> One voice alone can be heard:
> "Who is not for us is against us.
> There are no neutrals. Truth is with us."
> And I stand alone among them
> In the roaring flame and smoke
> And with all the strength that I have
> Say a prayer for them both.

Such words, as blasphemous as a simultaneous prayer to God and Satan, could not possibly be permitted. It was more correct to proclaim them to be a prayer to the Devil: "Who is not for us is against us." And this is what the new culture did. If it turned again toward the superfluous man, it was only to prove that he was not at all superfluous but rather harmful, dangerous, and negative.

Naturally, the leader of the new crusade was Gorki. In 1901 he sketched the first model of the positive hero and attacked those "who were born without faith in the heart," who "never felt that

---

been posthumously "rehabilitated" recently and her work republished.—TR.

anything was true," who "forever wandered between yes and no."

Gorki roared "No!" at these superfluous men, who roused his ire by their indefiniteness, and called them "petty bourgeois." Later he extended the concept of "petty bourgeois" far and wide and cast into it all who did not belong to the new religion: property owners large and small, liberals, conservatives, hooligans, humanists, decadents, Christians, Dostoevski, Tolstoi. Gorki was a man of *printsipialnost*; G. Chulkov called him the only truly believing writer of his time. He knew that all that is not God is Devil.

The literary revaluation of the superfluous man and his rapid transformation into a negative figure was intensified in the 1920s, the formative years of the positive hero. When they were placed side by side, it became obvious to everybody that there were no heroes without Purpose, but only heroes who were for or against the Purpose and that the superfluous man was, when all is said and done, a camouflaged enemy, a base traitor who should be unmasked and punished as quickly as possible.

Thus wrote Gorki in *The Life of Klim Samgin*, Fadeev in *The Debacle*, and many others. In *The Towns and the Years* Fedin purged his heart of the last drop of pity for the superfluous hero, formerly so enchanting. The only dissonant note was perhaps struck by Sholokhov in his *And Quiet Flows the Don*. Having shown the tragic fate of that superfluous man, Grigori Melekhov, he bade him an affectionate farewell. Since his hero belonged to the simple people and not the intelligentsia, it was possible to close an eye to Sholokhov's behavior. Today his novel is considered a model of socialist realism. But it is a model that, for obvious reasons, has found no imitators.

Meanwhile, other superfluous men, wishing to save their lives, renounced their past and duly transformed themselves into positive heroes. One of them recently said: "There is nothing in the world more disgusting than fence-sitters. . . . Yes, yes, I am a Red. A Red, the Devil take you." (Fedin's *An Extraordinary Year*, 1949.) The curse was addressed, of course, to the Whites.

Thus did the hero of nineteenth-century Russian literature perish ingloriously.

PART THREE

In its content and spirit, as in its central figure, socialist realism is much closer to the eighteenth century than to the nineteenth. Without realizing it, we jump over the heads of our fathers and revive the tradition of our grandfathers. Like ourselves, the eighteenth century had the idea of political purposefulness, the feeling of its own superiority, and a clear consciousness that "God is with us":

Hark, hark, O Universe,
To vict'ries beyond human power;
Listen, O astounded Europe,
To the exploits of these Russians.
Peoples, know and understand,
Believe ye that with us is God;
Believe that, aided by His hand,
A single Russian can defeat

All your abysmal evil forces.
Peoples, know this dread Colossus:
God is with us, so honor ye the Russian.

These verses of the eighteenth-century poet Derzhavin have a very contemporary ring, though the
language would, of course, need modernizing. Like
the socialist system, so eighteenth-century Russia
conceived of itself as the center of Creation. Inspired by the plenitude of its virtues—"self-created
and self-fortified"—it proclaimed itself as an example to all peoples and all eras. Its religious
self-conceit was so strong that it did not even admit the possibility of the existence of other norms
and ideals. In his *Portrait of Felitsa,* Derzhavin,
praising the ideal reign of Catherine II, expressed
the desire that

Peoples savage and remote,
Covered still with wool and scales,
Dressed only with leaf and bark,
And adorned with wings of birds,
Should all gather at Her throne,
Hear the gentle voice of Law,
So that tears should run in torrents
Down their swarthy, sunburned faces.
They should cry and understand
The bliss of living in our time,

196

Should abandon their equality,
And all subject be to Her.

Derzhavin simply cannot imagine that these "savages," the Huns, Finns and other peoples that surrounded the Russian throne somewhat in the manner of the International, should reject this flattering offer and not wish to submit at once to Catherine, who is, after all, "celestial grace incarnate." For him, as for our writers, anyone who does not wish to become like the model proposed to him and does not hasten to forget his barbarous "equality" and accept the proffered gift of "bliss" falls into one of two categories. He either is so stupid that he does not understand his own interests, in which case he must be re-educated; or he lacks virtue and is, to use one of our words, a "reactionary," in which case he must be liquidated. For in our world there is nothing finer than this state, this faith, this life, and this Empress. So Derzhavin believed, just as a contemporary poet who celebrates the new reign in Derzhavin's language:

There is no country like vast Russia,
No flowers grow as bright as ours,
Great is our people, free and deathless,
Our proud, eternal Russian people.
It stemmed attacking hordes of Batu

197

And broke all chains that held it down,
It made Russia and it raised her
To heights of stars and crests of time.

A. PROKOFIEV

Eighteenth-century literature produced its own positive hero. He is "the friend of common good"; he "strives to surpass all in courage," etc.; i.e., he constantly raises the level of his political morality, possesses all the virtues, and tells everybody just what to do. This literature knew nothing of the superfluous man. Neither did it know the destructive laughter that was the chronic disease of Russian culture from Pushkin to Blok and reached its climax among the decadents. "All the most lively and sensitive children of our century are stricken by a disease unknown to doctors and psychiatrists. It is related to the disorders of the soul and might be called 'irony.' Its symptoms are fits of an exhausting laughter which starts with a diabolic mockery and a provocative smile and ends as rebellion and sacrilege." (A. Blok, *Irony*, 1908.)

Seen in this way, irony is the laughter of the superfluous man who derides both himself and everything sacred in this world. "I know men who are ready to choke with laughter when they learn that their mother is dying, that they are starving to death, that their fiancée has betrayed them.

Through this accursed irony, everything is the same to them: good and evil, the blue sky and the stinking pit, Dante's Beatrice and Sologub's Untouchable Lady. [Fedor Sologub, a poet of the turn of the twentieth century, with decadent tendencies.] Everything is confused, as in a tavern or a fog." (Blok, *ibid.*)

Irony is the faithful companion of unbelief and doubt; it vanishes as soon as there appears a faith that does not tolerate sacrilege. There was no irony in Derzhavin, nor in Gorki—except for a few early tales. In Mayakovski there are a few examples, mostly from prerevolutionary times. Mayakovski soon found out what he could and what he could not laugh about. He could not permit himself to laugh at Lenin, whom he praised to the skies, any more than Derzhavin would laugh at his Empress. Pushkin, by contrast, addressed indecent verses even to the chaste and modest Tatiana. Pushkin was the first to taste the bitter joys of self-negation, even though he was gay and had a balanced character. As for Lermontov, he almost seems to have imbibed the poison in his childhood. In Blok himself and in his contemporaries Sologub and Leonid Andreev, destructive laughter became an elemental force sweeping everything before it.

As in the eighteenth century, we became severe and serious. This does not mean that we forgot how to laugh; but laughter ceased to be indecent and disrespectful; it acquired a Purpose. It eliminates faults, corrects manners, keeps up the brave spirits of youth. It is laughter with a serious face and with a pointing finger: "This is not the way to do things!" It is a laughter free from the acidity of irony.

Irony was replaced by pathos, the emotional element of the positive hero. We ceased to fear high-sounding words and bombastic phrases; we were no longer ashamed to be virtuous. The solemn eloquence of the ode suited us. We became classicists.

When Derzhavin, in his old age, wrote the ode "To the Great Boyar and Military Commander Reshemysl," he gave it a subtitle: "or the image of what a great lord should be." The art of socialist realism might be given the same subtitle: it represents the world and man as they should be.

Socialist realism starts from an ideal image to which it adapts the living reality. Our demand "to represent life truthfully in its revolutionary development" is really nothing but a summons to view truth in the light of the ideal, to give an ideal interpretation of reality, to present what should be as what is. For we interpret "revolutionary development" as the inevitable movement toward Communism, toward our ideal, in the light of which we see reality. We represent life as we would like it to be and as it is bound to become, when it bows to the logic of Marxism. This is why socialist realism should really be called "socialist classicism."

Some theoretical books and articles by Soviet writers and critics use the terms "romanticism" and "revolutionary romanticism." Gorki wrote much about the links between romanticism and socialist realism. He longed for "the illusion that exalts" and defended the artist's right to embellish life and to present it as better than it is. These calls did not remain unheeded, though many of Gorki's formulas are now veiled by an embarrassed silence or interpreted pharisaically: it is obviously not easy to admit that what we really need are some pretty lies. No, no, God forbid! We are against illusions and against idealization; we write only the truth and at the same time present life in its revolutionary development. Why should we embellish life? It is quite beautiful as it is, we are not out to embellish it, we just want to show the seeds of the future it contains. Romanticism is legitimate provided it does not conflict with realism. Revolutionary romanticism, like "revolutionary development" and "seeds of the future," is inherent in life, which, as inveterate romantics, we depict truthfully.

All this talk is merely our usual literary politics. In reality—as Gorki knew—romanticism suited our tastes only too well. It gravitates toward the ideal,

201

makes our wishes pass for the truth, likes pretty knickknacks, is not afraid of bombast. This is why it had its well-known success among us. Yet romanticism has played a less important part in our art than might have been expected. It made its presence felt mostly in the prehistory and initial period of socialist realism. In its mature period—the last twenty, thirty years—socialist realism has had a comparatively slight romantic tinge.

Romanticism is intimately connected with the *Sturm und Drang* period of Soviet literature, the first five years after 1917, when life and art were flooded with sentiment, when the blazing élan toward a happy future and the world-wide significance of the Revolution were not yet regimented by a strict political order. Romanticism is our past, our youth for which we long. It is the ecstasy of swollen banners, the explosions of passion and rage, the rattling of sabers and the neighing of horses, the shootings without judgment and without consequences, the "On to Warsaw!," the life, sleep, and death under the naked sky lit by the fires of regiments as nomadic as the Tartars of old:

> *Youth that led us*
> *To the march of sabers,*
> *Youth that threw us*
> *On the ice of Kronstadt.*

Battle horses
Carried us off,
On city squares
They massacred us.

E. BAGRITSKI

These are not just the sentiments of revolution-
ists who have survived and grown fat. The memory
of the Revolution is as sacred, both to those who
took part in it and to those who were born after it,
as the image of a dead mother. It is easier for us
to grant that everything that happened after the
Revolution was its betrayal than to insult its memory by reproaches and suspicions. Unlike the party,
the state, the Ministry of State Security, collectivization, Stalin, etc., the Revolution needs no justification by the Communist paradise that awaits us.
It is self-justified and justified emotionally, like
love or inspiration. And even though the Revolution was carried out in the name of Communism,
its name does not sound less sweet to us for that.
Maybe even sweeter. . . .

We live between past and future, between the
Revolution and Communism. And if Communism,
promising us golden mountains and representing
the inevitable logical outcome of all human history,
imperiously pulls us forward, the past too pushes
us in the back. For it is we who accomplished the

Revolution. How then can we blame it or blaspheme against it? We are caught in this psychological squeeze. In itself, we may like it or not. But both before us and behind us stand temples so splendid that we could not bear to attack them. And when we remember that, should our enemies win, they would make us return to the prerevolutionary mode of life (or incorporate us in Western democracy, it hardly matters), then, I am sure, we will start once more from where we began. We will start from the Revolution.

While working on this article I have caught myself more than once dropping into irony—that unworthy device! I caught myself trying to avoid the phrase "Soviet power." I preferred to use its synonyms, like "our state," "the socialist system" and so on. No doubt this was due to the fact that when I was young, the words of one of our Civil War songs went straight to my soul:

> All of us into the fight
> For Soviet power
> And as one man we'll die
> Fighting for it.

It is enough for me to pronounce the words "Soviet power" to make me see the Revolution with my mind's eye. I see the taking of the Winter Palace, the rattling motion of machine-gun belts, the bread cards for one-eighth of a pound, the defense of Red Petersburg. In a strictly logical judgment, "Soviet power" and "the socialist state" are the same thing. But if I have a few things against the socialist state—trifles, all of them—I have absolutely nothing against the Soviet power. Ridiculous? Maybe. But this is also romanticism.

Yes, we are all romantic with regard to our past. But the further away we are from our past and the closer we come to Communism, the weaker becomes the romantic halo that art has bestowed upon the Revolution. This is understandable: romanticism is, indeed, part of our nature; but it is not all of it. Sometimes it even violates our nature.

Romanticism is too anarchic and too emotional, while we are becoming ever more disciplined rationalists. It is at the mercy of turbulent feelings and diffuse moods, forgetting logic, common sense, and law. "The folly of the brave is the wisdom of life," the young Gorki assured us. This advice was timely when the Revolution was made: fools were necessary then. But can we call the Five-Year Plan "folly of the brave"? Or the guidance of the Party? Or, indeed, Communism itself, inevitably prepared by the logical course of history? Here every point is thought through, rationally foreseen, and subdivided into corresponding paragraphs. What folly is this? Hm, Comrade Gorki, you obviously haven't read your Marx!

Romanticism is powerless to express our clarity and precision. Composed gestures and even moderately solemn speech are foreign to it. It waves its arms, gets excited, and dreams distant dreams of the time when Communism is all but built and will be seen any moment.

In affirming an ideal, romanticism is not binding enough. It takes the wish for the reality. This is not bad in itself, but it smells of subjectivism and lack of self-restraint. The wish is the reality, because it must be. Our life is beautiful not only because we want it to be beautiful but also because it must be so: it has no choice.

All these arguments, mostly voiceless and unconscious, gradually dried up the hot current of romanticism. The river of art was covered with the ice of classicism. As art become more precise, rational, and teleological, it squeezed out romanticism.

The cold breath and ponderous heaviness of classicism were felt by us long ago, but few men dared to be outspoken on this subject. "The spirit of classicism blows upon us from all directions. All breathe it; but they either cannot distinguish it or don't know its name or simply are afraid to speak about it." (A. Efros, *The Messenger on the Doorstep,* 1922.)

The most daring of all was N. Punin, a fine art critic. At that time he was connected with futurism; he is completely forgotten now. As early as 1918 he noted "the marked classicism of Mayakovski's verses." He declared that in his *Mystery Bouffe*— his first major postrevolutionary work—Mayakovski "ceased to be a romanticist and became a classicist." He forecast that "much as he would like to, Mayakovski will never again rebel as impetuously as he did in the past."

Although his forecast proved remarkably correct —and not only as regards Mayakovski—the term "classicism" did not take hold in a Soviet literature that kept becoming more clearly classicist. It was, perhaps, too embarrassingly frank. Also, it recalled certain undesirable associations that seemed to lower our dignity. We preferred to call ourselves modestly "socialist realists" and hide our name under this pseudonym. Yet the great majority of our works, both good and bad, have the stamp of classicism, whether clear or obscure. It is apparent in the positive hero and in the strictly hierarchical distribution of the other roles, in plot and in language.

Beginning with the 1930s, the passion for solemnity finally imposes itself, and a pompous simplicity of style, the hallmark of classicism, becomes fashionable. We call our state "the Power"; the mujik, "cultivator of the bread"; the soldier, "the warrior"; the sword, "saber." We capitalize a great number of words. Allegorical figures and personified abstractions invade our literature, and we speak with slow solemnity and grandiose gestures.

> Yes, we believe, we must believe
> That truth exists—this is our stand;
> And that the good is not defenseless
> And conquers evil in the end.
>
> A. TVARDOVSKI

> The time has come! In vain with cruel fate
> The Fascist Lord has Moscow threatened long.
> But to victorious Moscow fell Berlin.
>
> M. ISAKOVSKI

The first heroes of Soviet literature stormed the fortresses of capitalism with torn bast shoes on their feet and sexual oaths on their lips. They were coarse and unrestrained: "Vanka! Put some paper rubles in your shoes! You can't scoot barefoot to the meeting!" (Mayakovski.) But now they have acquired good looks, elegant clothes, and refined manners. If they are sometimes lacking in taste, this is the national and social trait of our classicism, born as it was of Russian democracy. But neither the heroes nor their authors ever suspect that they are in bad taste. They try with all their power to be beautiful, polite, and cultured. They present every detail "correctly" and "in the best of taste."

"Under the white ceiling sparkled an elegant chandelier, fringed with transparent glass pendants, as with icicles . . . Tall silvery columns supported a blindingly white cupola, decorated with necklaces of electric bulbs."

What is this? A Tsar's palace? No, an ordinary club in a provincial town.

"On the stage, by the polished wing of the grand piano, stood Rakitin, dressed in sober gray. Like a blue river, a necktie flowed down his breast."

A singer? A fashionable tenor? No, a simple Party worker.

And now let's look at the people. They do not curse, they do not fight, they do not drink themselves senseless the way the Russian people used to do. And if they take a drink at a wedding table covered with exquisite foods, it is only as an accompaniment of toasts:

Terentii raised his eyes, looked around at the guests, rumblingly coughed into his fist, caressed the silver flow of his beard with a trembling hand, and said:

"First of all, let us congratulate the young couple. May they be happy and embellish the earth by their presence."

The guests followed him with their toasts, among the melodious clinking of the wine glasses:

"May they honor their parents!"

"May they have healthy children!"

"And not injure the glory of the kolkhoz!"

The quotation is taken from the novel *From the Whole Heart* by E. Maltsev, published in 1949. It is like dozens and hundreds of other novels. It is a sample of classicist prose of average literary quality. The style has long been a commonplace of our literature, and passes from author to author without undergoing any substantial change.

Every style has its distinctive quality. But classicism is more prone than other styles to impose its mark, to observe pedantically definite canons and norms, to be conservative as to form. It is among the most stable of styles. It brings and accepts new elements mostly in its formative period, but later tries to follow established models faithfully and is hostile to researches in form, experimentalism, and originality. This is why it rejected the talents of many poets who wanted to embrace it but retain their personalities: V. Khlebnikov, O. Mandelshtam,

210

and N. Zabolotski among them.[1] Even Mayakovski, whom Stalin called "the most talented poet of our Soviet era," remained a tragically solitary figure within it.

Mayakovski was too much of a revolutionary to become a traditionalist. To this day he is accepted politically rather than poetically. For all the paeans written to his glory, his rhythms, images, and language seem overbold to most of our poets. Those who want to follow in his footsteps copy his mannerisms but are unable to grasp what is essential in him—his boldness, inventiveness, and passion. They imitate his verses but don't follow his example. Whether it is because Mayakovski was the first budding classicist who, having no predecessors, broke new ground, whether it is because he caught the spirit of the times—both in Russia and in the world at large—and, being a romantic, wrote like an expressionist while combining his classicism with the constructivist style, or whether it is simply because he was a genius, his poetry is alive with the spirit of innovation, and this spirit left us when he died.

Geniuses, of course, are not born every day, and

[1] Khlebnikov, who died in 1922, was one of the founders of Russian futurism. Mandelshtam, who rebelled against the symbolists, died after deportation. Zabolotski is among the most talented Soviet poets today.—Tr.

the state of art rarely seems satisfactory to contemporaries. Still I must sadly confess, with others of my contemporaries, that our literature has become progressively impoverished in the last two or three decades. Fedin, Fadeev, Ehrenburg, Ivanov, and many others have written worse and worse with the years. The twenties, of which Mayakovski wrote: "Only poets, alas, we have none," now seem to be the years in which poetry flourished. Since the writers accepted socialist realism en masse—the beginning of the thirties—literature has gone down and down. Some few glimmers of light during the Patriotic War did not save it.

In this contradiction between the victory of socialist realism and the low quality of literary production, many are inclined to blame socialist realism. They say that great art cannot be written under it and even that it is the death of all art. But Mayakovski provides a refutation, to start with. For all the originality of his talents he remained an orthodox Soviet writer, perhaps the most orthodox Soviet writer—and this did not stop him from writing good poetry. He was an exception to general rules, but mostly because he observed these rules more strictly than others. In his poetic practice he carried out the demands of socialist realism more radically and more consistently. For the contradiction between socialist realism and literary quality,

212

the blame must fall on literature, i.e., on the writers who accepted the rules of socialist realism but did not have sufficient artistic consistency to embody them in deathless images. Mayakovski had that consistency.

Art is not afraid of dictatorship, severity, repressions, or even conservatism and clichés. When necessary, art can be narrowly religious, dumbly governmental, devoid of individuality—and yet good. We go into aesthetic raptures over the stereotypes of Egyptian art, Russian icons and folklore. Art is elastic enough to fit into any bed of Procrustes that history presents to it. But there is one thing it cannot stand: eclecticism.

Our misfortune is that we are convinced socialist realists but not convinced enough. Submitting to its cruel rules, we are yet afraid to follow to the end the road that we ourselves have chosen. No doubt, if we were less educated, it would be easier for us to attain the integrity that is indispensable to a writer. But we went to school, read all kinds of books, and learned only too well that there were great writers before us—Balzac, Maupassant, Tolstoi, and, yes, what's his name?—Chekhov. This is what has undone us. We wanted to become famous and to write like Chekhov. This unnatural liaison produced monsters.

It is impossible, without falling into parody, to

produce a positive hero in the style of full socialist realism and yet make him into a psychological portrait. In this way, we will get neither psychology nor hero. Mayakovski knew this and, hating psychological analysis and details, wrote in proportions that were larger than life. He wrote coarsely, poster-style, Homerically. He avoided like a plague descriptions of common life and rural nature. He broke with "the great traditions of great Russian literature" and, though he loved Pushkin and Chekhov, he did not try to imitate them. All this helped Mayakovski to lift himself to the level of his epoch and to express its spirit fully and clearly, without alien admixtures.

But the writing of so many other writers is in a critical state right now precisely because, in spite of the classicist nature of our art, they still consider it realism. They do it because they base their judgments on the literary criticism of the nineteenth century, which is furthest away from us and most foreign to us. Instead of following the road of conventional forms, pure fantasy, and imagination which the great religious cultures always took, they try to compromise. They lie, they maneuver, and they try to combine the uncombinable: the positive hero (who logically tends toward the pattern, the allegory) and the psychological analysis of character; elevated style and declamation with and prosaic descriptions of ordinary life; a high ideal with truthful representation of life.

The result is a loathsome literary salad. The characters torment themselves though not quite as Dostoevski's do, are mournful but not quite like Chekhov's, found their happy families which are not quite like Tolstoi's, and, suddenly becoming aware of the time they are living in, scream at the reader the copybook slogans which they read in Soviet newspapers, like "Long live world peace!" or "Down with the warmongers!" This is neither classicism nor realism. It is a half-classicist half-art, which is none too socialist and not at all realist.

It seems that the very term "socialist realism" contains an insoluble contradiction. A socialist, i.e., a purposeful, a religious, art cannot be produced with the literary method of the nineteenth century called "realism." And a really faithful representation of life cannot be achieved in a language based on teleological concepts. If socialist realism really wants to rise to the level of the great world cultures and produce its *Communiad*, there is only one way to do it. It must give up the "realism," renounce the sorry and fruitless attempts to write a socialist *Anna Karenina* or a socialist *Cherry Orchard*. When it abandons its effort to achieve verisimilitude, it will be able to express the grand and implausible sense of our era.

Unfortunately, this is not likely to happen. The events of the last few years have dragged our art on a road of half-measures and half-truths. The death of Stalin inflicted an irreparable loss upon our religiously aesthetic system; it cannot be resuscitated through the now revived cult of Lenin. Lenin is too much like an ordinary man and his image is too realistic: small, bald, dressed in civilian clothes. Stalin seemed to be specially made for the hyperbole that awaited him: mysterious, omniscient, all-powerful, he was the living monument of our era and needed only one quality to become God —immortality.

Ah, if only we had been intelligent enough to surround his death with miracles! We could have announced on the radio that he did not die but had risen to Heaven, from which he continued to watch us, in silence, no words emerging from beneath the mystic mustache. His relics would have cured men struck by paralysis or possessed by demons. And children, before going to bed, would have kneeled by the window and addressed their prayers to the cold and shining stars of the Celestial Kremlin.

But we did not listen to the voice of our conscience. Instead of intoning devout prayers, we set about dethroning the "cult of personality" that we ourselves had created. We thus blew up the foundations of that classicist colossus which, if we had waited but a little, would have joined the Pyramid of Cheops and the Apollo Belvedere in the treasury of world art.

The strength of a theological system resides in its constancy, harmony, and order. Once we admit that God carelessly sinned with Eve and, becoming jealous of Adam, sent him off to labor at land reclamation, the whole concept of the Creation falls apart, and it is impossible to restore the faith.

After the death of Stalin we entered upon a period of destruction and re-evalution. It is a slow and inconsistent process, it lacks perspective, and the inertia of both past and future lie heavy on it. Today's children will scarcely be able to produce a new God, capable of inspiring humanity into the next historical cycle. Maybe He will have to be supplemented by other stakes of the Inquisition, by further "personality cults," and by new terrestrial labors, so that after many centuries a new Purpose will rise above the world. But today no one yet knows its name.

And meanwhile our art is marking time between an insufficient realism and an insufficient classicism. Since the loss it suffered, it is no longer able to fly toward the ideal and to sing the praises of our life in a sincere and elevated style, presenting what should be as what is. In our works of glorification resound ever more openly the notes of baseness and hypocrisy. The most successful writers are those who can present our achievements as truthfully as possible and our failings as tactfully, delicately, and untruthfully as possible. Any works that lean too far toward an "excessive verisimilitude"—meaning realism—fail. This is what happened with Dudintsev's novel *Not by Bread Alone,* which stirred up a lot of noise and was publicly anathematized for blackening our bright socialist reality.

But is the dream of the old, good, and honest "realism" the only heresy to which Russian literature is susceptible? Is it possible that all the lessons that we received were taught in vain and that, in the best of cases, all we wish is to return to the naturalist school and the critical tendency? Let us hope that this is not so and that our need for truth will not interfere with the work of thought and imagination.

Right now I put my hope in a phantasmagoric art, with hypotheses instead of a Purpose, an art in which the grotesque will replace realistic descriptions of ordinary life. Such an art would correspond best to the spirit of our time. May the fantastic imagery of Hoffmann and Dostoevski, of Goya, Chagall, and Mayakovski (the most socialist realist of all), and of many other realists and nonrealists teach us how to be truthful with the aid of the absurd and the fantastic.

Having lost our faith, we have not lost our enthusiasm about the metamorphoses of God that take place before our very eyes, the miraculous transformations of His entrails and His cerebral convolutions. We don't know where to go; but, realizing that there is nothing to be done about it, we start to think, to set riddles, to make assumptions. May we thus invent something marvelous? Perhaps; but it will no longer be socialist realism.